Seven Crucial Conversations in Early Childhood Education

Where Have We Been and Why Does It Matter?

Edited By

Nancy File, Nancy E. Barbour, and
Andrew J. Stremmel

Foreword by Diane M. Horm

Teachers College Press
Teachers College | Columbia University
New York and London

Published by Teachers College Press,® 1234 Amsterdam Avenue, New York, NY 10027

Library of Congress Cataloging-in-Publication Data

Names: File, Nancy, editor. | Barbour, Nancy E., editor. | Stremmel, Andrew J., editor.

Title: Seven crucial conversations in early childhood education : where have we been and why does it matter? / edited by Nancy File, Nancy E. Barbour, and Andrew J. Stremmel; foreword by Diane M. Horm.

Description: New York : Teachers College Press, [2024] | Series: Early childhood education series | Includes bibliographical references and index. | Summary: "Influential leaders dialogue about how the field of early childhood education has changed over decades, helping us understand what is important for young children and families."—Provided by publisher.

Identifiers: LCCN 2023048402 (print) | LCCN 2023048403 (ebook) | ISBN 9780807769300 (paper : acid-free paper) | ISBN 9780807769317 (hardcover : acid-free paper) | ISBN 9780807782194 (ebook)

Subjects: LCSH: Early childhood education.

Classification: LCC LB1139.23 .S48 2024 (print) | LCC LB1139.23 (ebook) | DDC 372.21—dc23/eng/20231121

LC record available at https://lccn.loc.gov/2023048402

LC ebook record available at https://lccn.loc.gov/2023048403

ISBN 978-0-8077-6930-0 (paper)
ISBN 978-0-8077-6931-7 (hardcover)
ISBN 978-0-8077-8219-4 (ebook)

Printed on acid-free paper
Manufactured in the United States of America

Seven Crucial Conversations in Early Childhood Education: Where Have We Been and Why Does It Matter?
NANCY FILE, NANCY E. BARBOUR, & ANDREW J. STREMMEL, EDS.

Supporting Korean American Children in Early Childhood Education: Perspectives From Mother-Educators
SOPHIA HAN, JINHEE KIM, SOHYUN MEACHAM, & SU-JEONG WEE

Relationship-Based Care for Infants and Toddlers: Fostering Early Learning and Development Through Responsive Practice
SUSAN L. RECCHIA, MINSUN SHIN, & ELENI LOIZOU

Infants and Toddlers at Work: Using Reggio-Inspired Materials to Support Brain Development, Second Edition
ANN LEWIN-BENHAM

Leading Anti-Bias Early Childhood Programs: A Guide to Change, for Change, 2nd Ed.
LOUISE DERMAN-SPARKS, DEBBIE LEEKEENAN, & JOHN NIMMO

We Are the Change We Seek: Advancing Racial Justice in Early Care and Education
IHEOMA U. IRUKA, TONIA R. DURDEN, KERRY-ANN ESCAYG, & STEPHANIE M. CURENTON

Young Investigators: The Project Approach in the Early Years, 4th Ed.
JUDY HARRIS HELM, LILIAN G. KATZ, & REBECCA WILSON

Emotionally Responsive Teaching: Expanding Trauma-Informed Practice With Young Children
TRAVIS WRIGHT

Rooted in Belonging: Critical Place-Based Learning in Early Childhood and Elementary Teacher Education
MELISSA SHERFINSKI WITH SHARON HAYES

Transforming Early Years Policy in the U.S.: A Call to Action
MARK K. NAGASAWA, LACEY PETERS, MARIANNE N. BLOCH, & BETH BLUE SWADENER, EDS.

Music Therapy With Preschool Children on the Autism Spectrum: Moments of Meeting
GEOFF BARNES

On Being and Well-Being in Infant/Toddler Care and Education: Life Stories From Baby Rooms
MARY BENSON MCMULLEN

Principals as Early Learning Leaders: Effectively Supporting Our Youngest Learners
JULIE NICHOLSON, HELEN MANIATES, SERENE YEE, THOMAS WILLIAMS JR., VERONICA UFOEGBUNE, & RAUL ERAZO-CHAVEZ

Resisting the Kinder-Race: Restoring Joy to Early Learning
CHRISTOPHER P. BROWN

Reshaping Universal Preschool: Critical Perspectives on Power and Policy
LUCINDA GRACE HEIMER & ANN ELIZABETH RAMMINGER, WITH KATHERINE K. DELANEY, SARAH GALANTER-GUZIEWSKI, LACEY PETERS, & KRISTIN WHYTE

Pre-K Stories: Playing with Authorship and Integrating Curriculum in Early Childhood
DANA FRANTZ BENTLEY & MARIANA SOUTO-MANNING

Ready or Not: Early Care and Education's Leadership Choices—12 Years Later, 2nd Ed.
STACIE G. GOFFIN & VALORA WASHINGTON

Teaching STEM in the Preschool Classroom: Exploring Big Ideas with 3- to 5-Year-Olds
ALISSA A. LANGE, KIMBERLY BRENNEMAN, & HAGIT MANO

High-Quality Early Learning for a Changing World: What Educators Need to Know and Do
BEVERLY FALK

Guiding Principles for the New Early Childhood Professional: Building on Strength and Competence
VALORA WASHINGTON & BRENDA GADSON

Leading for Change in Early Care and Education: Cultivating Leadership from Within
ANNE L. DOUGLASS

When Pre-K Comes to School: Policy, Partnerships, and the Early Childhood Education Workforce
BETHANY WILINSKI

Continuity in Children's Worlds: Choices and Consequences for Early Childhood Settings
MELISSA M. JOZWIAK, BETSY J. CAHILL, & RACHEL THEILHEIMER

For a complete list of series titles, visit https://www.tcpress.com/ece

continued

Early Childhood Education Series, *continued*

The Early Intervention Guidebook for Families and Professionals, 2nd Ed.
BONNIE KEILTY

STEM Learning with Young Children
SHELLY COUNSELL ET AL.

Courageous Leadership in Early Childhood Education
SUSI LONG ET AL., EDS.

Teaching Kindergarten
JULIE DIAMOND ET AL., EDS.

The New Early Childhood Professional
VALORA WASHINGTON ET AL.

Teaching and Learning in a Diverse World, 4th Ed.
PATRICIA G. RAMSEY

In the Spirit of the Studio, 2nd Ed.
LELLA GANDINI ET AL., EDS.

Exploring Mathematics Through Play in the Early Childhood Classroom
AMY NOELLE PARKS

Becoming Young Thinkers
JUDY HARRIS HELM

The Early Years Matter
MARILOU HYSON & HEATHER BIGGAR TOMLINSON

Thinking Critically About Environments for Young Children
LISA P. KUH, ED.

Standing Up for Something Every Day
BEATRICE S. FENNIMORE

FirstSchool
SHARON RITCHIE & LAURA GUTMANN, EDS.

Early Childhood Education for a New Era
STACIE G. GOFFIN

Everyday Artists
DANA FRANTZ BENTLEY

Multicultural Teaching in the Early Childhood Classroom
MARIANA SOUTO-MANNING

Inclusion in the Early Childhood Classroom
SUSAN L. RECCHIA & YOON-JOO LEE

Moral Classrooms, Moral Children, 2nd Ed.
RHETA DEVRIES & BETTY ZAN

Defending Childhood
BEVERLY FALK, ED.

Starting with Their Strengths
DEBORAH C. LICKEY & DENISE J. POWERS

The Play's the Thing
ELIZABETH JONES & GRETCHEN REYNOLDS

Twelve Best Practices for Early Childhood Education
ANN LEWIN-BENHAM

Big Science for Growing Minds
JACQUELINE GRENNON BROOKS

What If All the Kids Are White? 2nd Ed.
LOUISE DERMAN-SPARKS & PATRICIA G. RAMSEY

Seen and Heard
ELLEN LYNN HALL & JENNIFER KOFKIN RUDKIN

Connecting Emergent Curriculum and Standards in the Early Childhood Classroom
SYDNEY L. SCHWARTZ & SHERRY M. COPELAND

Infants and Toddlers at Work
ANN LEWIN-BENHAM

Educating and Caring for Very Young Children, 2nd Ed.
DORIS BERGEN ET AL.

Beginning School
RICHARD M. CLIFFORD & GISELE M. CRAWFORD, EDS.

Emergent Curriculum in the Primary Classroom
CAROL ANNE WIEN, ED.

Enthusiastic and Engaged Learners
MARILOU HYSON

Powerful Children
ANN LEWIN-BENHAM

Supervision in Early Childhood Education, 3rd Ed.
JOSEPH J. CARUSO WITH M. TEMPLE FAWCETT

Guiding Children's Behavior
EILEEN S. FLICKER & JANET ANDRON HOFFMAN

The War Play Dilemma, 2nd Ed.
DIANE E. LEVIN & NANCY CARLSSON-PAIGE

Playing to Get Smart
ELIZABETH JONES & RENATTA M. COOPER

The Emotional Development of Young Children, 2nd Ed.
MARILOU HYSON

Young Children Continue to Reinvent Arithmetic—2nd Grade, 2nd Ed.
CONSTANCE KAMII

Bringing Learning to Life
LOUISE BOYD CADWELL

Bringing Reggio Emilia Home
LOUISE BOYD CADWELL

Contents

Foreword

At the beginning of their introductory chapter, the editors note that this is a book about the history of early childhood education (ECE). They then immediately acknowledge that "history" may evoke connotations of lists of names and dates conveyed as discrete timelines of important people and their unique contributions, often devoid of information about the larger contexts and the interrelationships, experiences, and perceptions of the people shaping the history. This book takes a decidedly different and much more engaging approach. *Seven Crucial Conversations* embraces the notion that history is personal and uses the power of dialogue among those who shaped the history to reflect upon and discuss its unfolding over the last several decades.

The editors, adopting an unconventional and unique approach, acknowledge this book is written "outside of the typical academic style." First, the editors identified seven major topics and used these to organize the book as opposed to the name, date, contribution method. These topics—including systems of early care and education, diversity and equity, developmentally appropriate practice, play, curriculum and pedagogy, infant/toddler programming, and families and family engagement—are key topics in ECE over the last 50 to 70 years. Beyond using key, important topics in ECE's recent history as the main organizers of the book, the editors decided on a novel method to convey the history in these areas. They invited leaders who shaped the ECE field to engage in semi-structured dialogues about the evolution and development of the topics. Specifically, for each of the seven topics, two influential leaders who are recognized experts on it engage in back-and-forth conversations in response to open-ended prompts. As a result, the reader is sharing their perceptions of how the topic changed and evolved since the 1950s and 1960s. I often experienced the sense that I was listening in on the conversation of two professional friends as they reflected and discussed our field—generally not a perception associated with the reading of a history book! Each of these seven dialogues or conversations is followed by a reflective essay written by one of the editors to extend, highlight, and reinforce the salient points. This overall organization by key topic with the use of conversations to present the historical information accentuated by the editors' reflections makes one feel like they are getting the inside scoop on the growth and development of our field!

Although this book is about ECE's history, it is also about the future. Along with the editors, the authors adopted the stance of looking back and reflecting to provide insights, enhance understanding, and identify missed opportunities to note future challenges and needs to move the field forward. As a reader, I sensed the authors' enthusiasm of looking back and reflecting, often with a critical eye, to inform the future. Their joint reflections and dialogue provide important insights for the future of ECE.

Beyond the unique and engaging method of presenting history, the focus on ECE's relatively recent history, the last 50 to 70 years, also sets this book apart. Many ECE history books either do not cover, or give light coverage to, the period since the 1970s. The editors also offer discussion questions and resource lists for further reading as part of their commentary at the end of each dialogue. The books and articles listed as resources include seminal works that ECE students and professionals should know. These features make *Seven Crucial Conversations* a perfect textbook for both undergraduate- and graduate-level ECE courses focused on the history of our field. As a faculty member who teaches this type of course at the doctoral level, I plan to use this book in the future.

I invite you to read this book. I trust that, like me, you will find it to be an engaging and insightful history of ECE through the eyes of leaders who shaped the field. Together with the reflections of a mid-career colleague who provided a chapter with a focus on the challenges ahead, I found the book leaving me celebrating our successes with a renewed dedication to addressing our challenges in the years ahead.

—Diane M. Horm
Director, Early Childhood Education Institute (ECEI)
GKFF Endowed Chair and Professor of Early Childhood Education
David L. Boren Professor
The University of Oklahoma-Tulsa

Seven Crucial Conversations in Early Childhood Education

Introduction

Nancy File, Nancy E. Barbour, and Andrew J. Stremmel

This is a book about early childhood education's history, and we understand that the word "history" may not engender a sense of enthusiasm. Likely, most individuals have had unfortunate experiences with presentations of names, dates, and events that become hard to juggle en masse and do not, on their own, create a sense of meaning. That is not our focus. This is also a book about the future. One important reason for looking back is to establish firmer ideas about how to look and move forward. Our goal is to understand where the field of early childhood education has been in the last several decades. How has that mattered to the field both then and now, in the present? And what ideas can we draw about what the field needs in the future to serve all young children and their families well?

Why have we chosen to concentrate on the last several decades of history? Practice in early childhood education (ECE) in the United States can be traced back well over a century and a half to multiple initiatives—the kindergarten movement; infant schools and care for the children of industrial workers; the nursery school; laboratory schools located within university settings; and the settlement house movement, for example. These roots are disparate and often functioned separately from one another.

On the other hand, early childhood education, as we recognize its current profile, has a rather recent history. Over the last 6 to 7 decades the field of early childhood education has become more unified around its definition of serving young children from birth to age 8 and their families, although still across several different program auspices. At the same time, with kindergarten and now prekindergarten becoming entrenched within the public school system and with the growth in numbers of employed mothers, it is the case that this field of early childhood education is widespread and firmly anchored in American society.

This period of recent history has occurred in the context of particular cultural values. Noted by Chambers (1958) at the start of this critical era, there was a dominant belief that "America's mission was to lead the world in the unfolding of an ever finer tomorrow, the direction of history, in America at least, was onward and upward" (p. 197). Any orientation of values is marked by promises and pitfalls. Potential weaknesses of the "onward and upward" orientation are that ideas grow out of favor merely because a new idea has been posited and that we spend too little time examining what has been left behind as well as gained. The promise is that new ideas may rectify blind spots or provide necessary adjustments to changing societal expectations.

This book, then, encompasses slices of history from the last several decades in early childhood education. It was birthed across conversations among the three of us. We realized how much had changed across our decades of serving as early childhood professionals. We also realized that those who hadn't lived through this period may not be aware of the shifts in theory and practice, even in a relatively brief span of time.

The most meaningful history to us exists at the most personal level. What have been the experiences of those who helped to shape the field over the last several decades? We want to get closer to the discussion, shared beliefs, and even possible lack of agreement that occurred among people, including consideration at the time, and in retrospect, of what might be successes, letdowns, and missed opportunities. We also hold a strong belief in the power of dialogue, and so we asked our contributors to have a conversation with each other. What is recorded in this book is different than any one of our contributors could write on their own, via the dialogue. Being in on the action as two people share their thoughts allows readers to begin to create their own stake in what is being discussed. We believe that taking stock and making change in the field is most fruitful when these efforts take place within dialogue.

This book contains seven conversations, each one focused on a major topic area within the field: the systems of early care and education; diversity, equity, and children's rights; the National Association of Young Children's position statement on developmentally appropriate practice; the place of play; curriculum and pedagogy; the place of infants and toddlers; and families and family engagement.

Our contributors have spent decades working within those topic areas. For each conversation we posed four open-ended questions to give the contributors a place to start. Nonetheless, the conversations took their own direction as they came to life. The questions are reproduced within the chapters, and they invited contributors to go back to the beginning of their careers as well as envision the future.

In addition, each conversation has these features:

- Brief biographies of the contributors appear at the start of each chapter to allow readers to understand their earned status as experts.
- Following each conversation, one of the editors provides a reflective essay. We use this space to provide background information, emphasize connections, and initiate the process of making meaning of the conversation. Of course, the essay is only one possible reflection on the conversations, and we urge readers to consider their own ways to make meaning.
- We provide discussion questions. These are a beginning, and we anticipate that readers will find their own points of interest and questions.
- A short list of articles and books is provided for those interested in further reading.

Finally, we asked our contributors to write in a conversational, rather than academic, style. Readers will not find citations and references within the conversations, but it is possible to locate any documents being discussed via online search tools. Any material contained in brackets was added by the editors to assist readers in this effort.

Readers will form their own perspectives about what these conversations mean for the field. As for next steps forward, we believe that these are best determined within their own time and place. What these conversations mean for the future will be impacted in part by what happens between the time they were written and when they are read, in addition to interpretations of what they mean.

We end with a reflective chapter written by a colleague in the middle of her career. We've asked her to consider what the conversations mean to her work within the field. Her own sense of meaning is a beginning point for readers to reflect upon their applications of the conversations.

To close, as a group we offer our most sincere thanks to our contributors. We are incredibly grateful that they joined us on an adventure in writing outside of the typical academic style. We note that they contributed equally to the work, and authorship is alphabetical.

Nancy File acknowledges the young children she taught, who shaped so much of what she knows and values. Similarly, students in teacher preparation have been a source of inspiration. Colleagues who have worked alongside her and at other institutions enabled her professional growth and offered the sustenance of friendship. Her husband, children, and young grandchildren are at the heart of it all.

Nancy Barbour acknowledges her career-long interest in the history of child development and early childhood education that began with her doctoral dissertation. She sees the place of history as essential to understanding future directions. She also acknowledges the children, students, and colleagues who have influenced her thinking over so many years. She is grateful for the love and support of her husband in the pursuit of her work.

Andy acknowledges the many children, student teachers, mentors, and colleagues who gave him his best education. Each, in their own way, helped him to view conversation as the means to open new perspectives, create new understandings, and embrace learning that is more authentic and primarily about human development. He also is grateful to his wife and children for their continuing support.

REFERENCE

Chambers, C. A. (1958). The belief in progress in twentieth-century America. *Journal of the History of Ideas, 19*, 197–224.

CHAPTER 1

Systems of Early Care and Education

W. Steven Barnett and Jacqueline Jones

W. Steven Barnett is a Board of Governors Professor of Education and founding Co-Director of the National Institute for Early Education Research (NIEER) at Rutgers University. Dr. Barnett is an economist who conducted groundbreaking cost-benefit analyses of the Perry Preschool and Abecedarian programs. His research has covered many other aspects of early childhood education policy for children from birth to age 5. He has led multiple large-scale evaluations of public early childhood education initiatives and their long-term effects, including a study of New Jersey's court-mandated preschool program's impacts through high school. Dr. Barnett also developed the State of Preschool survey that has provided detailed data on every state's preschool policies continuously since 2002. Recent research includes national surveys of parents to assess the pandemic's impacts on preschool program participation, home learning activities, and social-emotional development of young children.

Jacqueline Jones is the former president and CEO of the Foundation for Child Development. Dr. Jones served as Deputy Assistant Secretary for Policy and Early Learning in the U.S. Department of Education. Prior to federal service, she was the Assistant Commissioner for the Division of Early Childhood Education in the New Jersey State Department of Education. Dr. Jones worked for over 15 years as a senior research scientist at the Educational Testing Service in Princeton. She has been a visiting faculty member at the Harvard Graduate School of Education and a full-time faculty member at the City University of New York. Dr. Jones has served on numerous national advisory committees, including the National Academies of Science, Engineering and Medicine's Board on Children Youth and Families and the Division of Behavioral and Social Sciences and Education. She received both M.A. and Ph.D. degrees from Northwestern University.

AT THE START AND THROUGHOUT YOUR CAREER, HOW DID YOU DEFINE ECE SYSTEMS? WHAT HAS BEEN THE RANGE OF THESE SYSTEMS?

STEVE: When I started to study the impacts of early childhood education (ECE), I was completing a Ph.D. in labor economics, and Urie Bronfenbrenner had just published *The Ecology of Human Development*. In a way, Bronfenbrenner had recreated and integrated the political economy and microeconomics of human development and the family with the framework of developmental psychology. I was fascinated by this, and the way I have thought of ECE systems has been very much influenced by my own combining of economic theories of supply and demand and their underpinning economic theories of individual and family behavior with Bronfenbrenner's ecological model.

From this economic/human ecology perspective, ECE systems include family, friends, and neighbors, as well as public and private providers of all kinds of early care and education, including Head Start, public schools, private schools, child care centers, and family child care homes. Decisions about parental and nonparental care and education for young children are made jointly by parents, and these decisions and their consequences interact so that the effects of home and out-of-home experiences on child development cannot be understood independently of each other. This complex ECE system is self-organizing and not centrally guided and controlled by anyone, though governments take actions to organize and fund parts of the system and intervene in significant ways that affect markets and other institutions, including families and family formation. This perspective led me to think about both individual-level and systems-level policy interventions with home and out-of-home environments to support learning and development with the goal of helping individuals and our society (communities, states, nations) to maximize their well-being.

The interdependence of home and out-of-home experiences emphasized by Bronfenbrenner has implications for research as well as policy. Perhaps the most critical implication for research is that if we want to understand either the developmental impacts of home environment and parenting *or* the developmental impacts of nonparental care and education such as Head Start or the number of years of child care prior to kindergarten, home, and out-of-home experiences, we should study them together. Except for randomized controlled trials (RCTs), studies of only one part of the system (home or out-of-home—e.g., preschool) are prone to bias, and RCTs have an array of limitations that are too often ignored.

Unfortunately, the ECE field seems to have paid little attention to this implication of Bronfenbrenner's work, though some researchers continued to emphasize the importance of understanding interactions between home/family and ECE outside the home. Much of the research on parenting and the family has largely ignored research on nonparental ECE except for research on parenting programs. Much of the research on the impacts of ECE programs has largely ignored the family and home environment, with most studies using statistical analysis to "control" for race, education, and income, what Bronfenbrenner referred to as using "social addresses." These social address variables fall far short of accurately delineating children's experiences in the home.

Returning to policy implications, another result of failing to absorb the lessons from Bronfenbrenner's work has been that the ECE field's vision of an ECE "system" has tended to be restricted to nonparental ECE and sometimes just to the government-funded or government-regulated sectors. I don't believe the seriousness of the incomplete picture of the environments supporting early learning and development has been fully acknowledged. For example, the term "child care desert" is frequently applied to areas with little or no publicly funded or subsidized ECE, without evidence that parents have not chosen parental care or informal nonparental care over the formal ECE alternatives or even that these formal ECE arrangements would provide better support for learning and development. Of course, parental choice is limited by income and other constraints, and some formal ECE arrangements provide stronger developmental support than some nonformal arrangements, but I suggest that these ECE ecologies are much more complex than "deserts." I worry that this kind of tunnel vision too often leads toward conceptualizing the ideal policy solution as a government-funded, centrally controlled, seamless organization of care and education rather than as a self-organizing system with families at the center. Indeed, such a self-organizing system often is referred to as a "nonsystem."

The perspective I set out above might seem contradictory coming from someone who promotes free, universal preschool education as a key policy solution to support stronger and more equitable supports for early learning and development. Others have taken the self-organizing market perspective I put forward as a justification for ECE vouchers. Much of my research has illuminated the sources of market failure—including highly imperfect information, societal spillovers from improvements in early learning and development, and financial constraints—as well as the highly unequal resources families are able to invest. At the same time, I think more attention should be given to policies that would provide substantial income transfers to parents of very young children. These policies are not mutually exclusive, and policies that increase supports for families and policies that directly increase access to high-quality nonparental ECE need to be developed and evaluated together.

JACQUELINE: Steve, I'm fascinated by your entry point into ECE; my own is quite different. I began my career studying the continuum of language development and breakdown, from early childhood to adolescence and adulthood. However, it was at Educational Testing Service (ETS) that I began working in ECE with a group of researchers who were conducting micro-level studies of young children's learning. We collaborated with early childhood classroom teachers to identify and implement effective strategies to document young children's literacy and science learning. Initially, we focused solely on the classroom and the classroom teacher, but it soon became apparent that a true understanding of children's learning required understanding beyond the classroom and the school. We needed information from and participation with the multitude of adults with whom the child was interacting. So, Bronfenbrenner was right! We quickly realized that if a complete picture of children's learning was to emerge, there had to be multiple forms of evidence of children's learning from multiple sources and that teachers needed to develop genuine community-wide partnerships with parents, grandparents, other caretakers, and educational, medical, and social services professionals.

My colleagues and I also understood that even the most dedicated teachers needed the support of school- and district-level administrators. Teachers needed administrators to acknowledge that young children's learning is complex and that the professionals charged with the design and implementation of curriculum and assessment strategies themselves require a good deal of time to engage in ongoing and high-quality professional learning opportunities. My ETS colleague Ted Chittenden believed that sound assessment of young children's learning should be based on the premise that it is not the young child's responsibility to tell adults what he or she knows. Rather, it is the adult's responsibility to create the environments and experiences in which children can demonstrate their knowledge, skills, and development. At the school and district levels, a successful program required time for teachers to create appropriate environments, collect evidence of children's learning, interpret that evidence, and translate the findings into effective instructional approaches. This level of administrative support for classroom teachers is essential. However, it remains quite rare.

When I found myself leading New Jersey's statewide preschool initiative, my notion of systems was forced to expand again. State policies and regulations could bump against federal regulations as well as local policies. I remember an occasion on which a school district superintendent wanted to have a centralized registration for all preschoolers, regardless of funding streams. He wanted to have Head Start children in the same classroom with children whose parents had higher incomes. His motives were right. Why should all the poor children be bundled together? However, at that time, this approach would have prevented the local Head Start grantee from meeting the required number of federally eligible attendees for their program. Their entire Head Start grant would have been in jeopardy. Federal regulations were in direct conflict with a well-intentioned local policy; the feds won. I never forgot that sinking feeling when we all realized that these systems were in conflict in ways that did not serve the best interest of young children.

In New Jersey's program that targeted 3- and 4-year-olds, the disjunctions between preschool and birth–3 and K–2 were also striking. Although we spent a good deal of time trying to link the preschool and K–12 standards, I still regret not being able to make strong linkages to the 0–3 space. Steve, the "nonsystem" to which you referred was apparent.

My work at the federal level brought these disconnects into full focus and brought us back to a more place-based approach. Since early childhood programs in the United States receive the bulk of their funding from the federal government under programs such as the Child Care Development Block Grant (CCDBG), Title I, Head Start, and the Individuals with Disabilities Education Act (IDEA), coordination at the federal level is essential. However, the major federal programs live across the Education Department and the Department of Health and Human Services and have different reauthorizations, regulations, and requirements. This makes meaningful coordination a challenge. I was thrilled to work with the staff designing the early childhood component for the Promise Neighborhoods program. Based on the model of the Harlem Children's Zone, this work captured the notion of the essential role of community in helping children reach their full potential. So my notion of ECE systems has followed a trajectory from individual teachers to national impact, and back to a community focus.

STEVE: That is fascinating, Jacqueline. Your points about policy incoherence are well taken. Given the serious market (I use this term to include the organization of both informal family, friend, and neighbor ECE as well fee-based formal arrangements) imperfections and the major role of government in ECE, the capacity for coherent self-organization is limited, and the problem of policy conflicts is substantial. The policy conflict problem is exacerbated by silos within and across levels of government, though we must recognize that silos are required for agency functioning and not just arbitrary organizational structures that can be abandoned without consequences. In ECE, federal policy does not align with state policy. State agencies conflict with one another. Local agencies, including city governments and school districts, have their own policies and differing interpretations of state and federal policies.

The importance of this policy incoherence is evident in the problems you noted, Jacqueline, including the problems of developing consistent policy and practice across the early childhood age span and across agencies serving children at the same ages. These include poor alignment between preschool and school regarding expectations for learning and teaching. This includes curriculum and inattention to supporting, rather than disrupting, programs for infants and toddlers when child care programs become part of the public education system providing preschool education. To take another very real concrete example from our own state of New Jersey, one state agency is currently providing funding to build new child care centers with room size standards that will not allow them to participate in the "mixed delivery" of state-funded preschool, the planned expansion of which will require hundreds of new classrooms.

WHAT EXTERNAL FORCES HAVE AFFECTED ECE SYSTEMS OVER YOUR CAREER?

STEVE: External forces include the social, economic, and policy trends that led to a large increase in single-parent families and in maternal labor market participation through the mid-1990s. Somewhat counter to what one might expect, after the welfare reform act of 1996, the Personal Responsibility and Work Opportunity Act, maternal employment rates ceased climbing and have remained at about the same level in the 2 decades since 2000. Unsurprisingly, ECE program participation (including all kinds of center-based programs) also remained about the same level—just 50 percent for ages 3 and 4—from the mid-1990s up to the pandemic. That there was virtually no change in ECE participation rates at ages 3 and 4 despite the changes in public policies over that more-than-2-decade span suggests both how important other factors are in determining ECE participation and how modest the impacts of our ECE policies have been. The net effect of national, state, and local policy progress has been a modest shift in young children from private fee-paid to publicly funded programs since the mid-1990s and almost no change in participation. By far the biggest impact in the past 2 decades was the COVID-19 pandemic, which greatly reduced participation rates in 2020, though there was a partial bounceback in 2021. Data that NIEER collected late in 2022 suggest we may be back to prepandemic participation levels, but perhaps not for children in the lowest-income families, a disturbing exception. The pandemic has been a shocking reminder that the past is not always a good guide to the future. Other external forces include the tendency for public ECE policies—especially at the federal level—to have been primarily to support means-tested programs for children in economically disadvantaged families. The recent development of universal programs in some states and cities is not yet a major influence nationally.

Several external forces may help to explain why the nation has not made more progress toward expanding ECE participation in the 21st century. One is that the federal government's role in education is largely limited to serving as an equalizer for children in poverty. The young child poverty rate has cycled up and down over the past 2 decades but did not exceed a quarter of children before hitting a low of 15% in 2019. This limited how much impact federal policy could have. Another is that advocacy has focused primarily on child care rather than education, but the parental demand for nonparental care to support employment has not increased. Changes in work arrangements during and after the pandemic may have reduced demand for child care further for segments of the population. Finally, policy incoherence may have contributed to the relative stasis to the extent that Head Start reduced the numbers of children served as states expanded the numbers of children served but with no truly collaborative approach to ensuring coverage of the populations Head Start and state programs were designed to serve. I am all too frequently reminded of a story Dr. Ed Zigler (a researcher and advocate credited as a key developer of the Head Start program) told me about his early days in Washington, DC, when he announced to a mentor that he was going to a meeting on collaboration. His mentor's response was something like, "That's great, are they going to collaborate you or are you going to collaborate them?"

The field should be concerned that while public policies have greatly increased the percentage of young children in publicly funded ECE programs, about half the 3- and 4-year-olds in poverty are still not in any classroom, public or private. Undoubtedly, there are benefits from higher-quality standards and from shifting the cost burden from parents to taxpayers, but far too many children remain unserved, especially in low- and middle-income families. Apparently, our policies have accomplished far less than might have been expected from the investments made. Perhaps our ECE policies have increased the quality of ECE, but how much and for whom is not well understood. The last nationally representative study of ECE quality was conducted for the Early Childhood Longitudinal Study, Birth Cohort (ECLS-B) in 2005 and found generally low levels of quality, though somewhat better in public than in private programs.

JACQUELINE: Steve, I certainly agree that social, economic, and policy forces have shaped ECE policy. Social policies such as the Great Society of the 1960s led to the design and implementation of Head Start. However, many ECE programs were developed and implemented through a "compensatory" lens that can carry a perception of the target children as "culturally, linguistically, and economically deprived," "disadvantaged," "deficient," and "limited." Often with good intentions, these programs might seek to make up for what the target population of children are perceived to be lacking. At best, the programs work to form strong partnerships with parents and communities. At worst, they view families and communities as devoid of any intrinsic value and a hindrance to children's healthy development.

Steve, we started this conversation with Bronfenbrenner. My fear is that negative perceptions of the young children themselves and the communities in which they live have potential to cloud Bronfenbrenner's ecological model and preclude our ability to include family, friends, neighbors, and so on as vital components of the ECE systems. A significantly damaging outcome has been the imposition of a skills-based rather than an inquiry-based curriculum in programs for children living in poverty. I hope that a universal notion of ECE would promote a sound curriculum that helps ECE professionals lead all children to their full potential. The High Quality Early Learning Project run by Dr. Beverly Falk at City College of the City University of New York provides a collection of video sets that demonstrate what high-quality early learning looks like from birth through 2nd grade in public school settings with children of varied economic backgrounds.

Perhaps my early work in schools with classroom teachers also leads me to the belief that administrative leadership is critical to any system, and the stability of good leadership plays a key role. Districts have thrived with consistent leadership. For example, I believe that Boston Public Schools' successful work has greatly benefited from having Jason Sachs's leadership for over 15 years. The South Brunswick, NJ, school district engaged in widely recognized and innovative work such as the district-wide Early Literacy Portfolio with over 20 years of Willa Spicer's leadership. There is no denying the challenges and negative impact of frequent turnover of high-level administrative staff.

In addition, there are sociocultural notions that hinder the development of comprehensive ECE systems. Those legislators who argue that "those babies should be home with their mamas" not only refute the documented numbers of working mothers, and the percentages of those whose paychecks are essential to support the family, but they impede the development of a robust set of experiences that could optimize children's learning and development at its most critical period. However, Steve, there are dangerous culture wars raging even as we engage in this conversation. I had hoped that early childhood education could remain above the political fray, but the governor of Alabama's ousting of that state's Secretary of the Department of Early Childhood Education in April 2023 because she would not disavow the National Association for the Education of Young Children's (NAEYC) [2022] text *Developmentally Appropriate Practice* (DAP) is extremely disturbing. This foundational guide for teachers was accused of promoting a "woke" agenda that taught about white privilege and structural racism, and promoted "equality, dignity and worth" around LGBTQ identities. According to the governor's office, the book contained material that focused on ideas such as the existence of a "larger systemic force that perpetuates systems of White privilege," and that "the United States is built on systemic and structural racism." DAP's section on structural racism states that "systemic and structural racism . . . has permeated every institution and system through policies and practices that position people of color in oppressive, repressive, and menial positions. The early education system is not immune to these forces." The resource also states that "Early childhood programs also serve and welcome families that represent many compositions. Children from all families (e.g., single parent, grandparent-led, foster, LGBTQIA+) need to hear and see messages that promote equality, dignity, and worth," the book states. It says that preschool is one place where children "begin to see how they are represented in society" and that the classroom should be a place of "affirmation and healing" [see npr.org].

We will see how these highly organized and heavily funded movements to suppress social justice efforts play out. However, I think the field must be ready to play a long game, which includes organizing and strategizing to ensure that the ECE field is committed to providing high-quality early experiences that help all children to reach their full potential and buffer all children against the harmful consequences of poverty, racism, prejudice, and discrimination. I hope we're up to the task.

STEVE: Jacqueline, I share your concerns. There is a constant threat that ECE will become a partisan political football and that ECE policy can be damaged in future culture wars as it has in the past. An earlier form of the culture wars sank the 1971 bipartisan federal legislation to establish a universal child care program. Politicians use fear to motivate voters, and parents are particularly vulnerable to fears about the nurturing of their young children. That makes ECE an appealing target in the culture wars, and I agree that we should expect ECE to be embroiled in the culture wars, and it is important to develop strategies for a long game. In a few states, the culture wars likely have stymied progress in expanding access to ECE altogether, for example, in those that currently do not provide state-funded preschool programs.

Racism and its consequences—including the undermining of social cohesion and trust that are essential to developing and implementing strong ECE polices—constitute one of the greatest challenges we face in education. Unfortunately, in taking on the essential work of antiracism, NAEYC made unforced errors that put ECE into a weak position in the culture wars. Specifically, it incorporated an indefensible position using language connotating a radical leftist ideological stance into their guide to developmentally appropriate practice (DAP). In my view, this unnecessarily alienated potential supporters and promoted a false narrative that systemic and structural racism is pervasive in *every institution* in America. Our institutions have always been more complex than that and included antiracist and equalitarian values. By failing to recognize this complexity, NAEYC put those espousing DAP in an indefensible position, made ECE an easier target in the culture wars, and allowed opponents to shift the focus away from racism and racial inequity to political ideology.

Mention of LBGTQIA+ in the NAEYC document and NAEYC's various publications on the topic should have been expected to draw ECE into the culture wars. Addressing issues of gender identity in preschool classrooms is complicated by the very different feelings, values, and perspectives among parents regarding gender identity and expression. More attention is needed to developing strategies to protect ECE policy and practice from inaccurate and misleading attacks on these issues and to defending appropriate practice. Particularly in ECE, there must be strategies to win over parents and policymakers (or at least enough of them). Greater success might be achieved by more proactive open engagement and discussion with parents and policymakers rather than trying to fly under the radar. One of my worries is that when those trying to seek political advantage by frightening parents are the first to engage with the public, they define our positions and practices in ways that are misleading and inaccurate and put the field on the defensive.

Turning to the concern that public programs have often had a deficit perspective, I want to clarify that this has different meanings depending on who uses the term. When I started in the field, it was common for economists—and others—to believe that cognitive abilities and perhaps also "noncognitive" or affective characteristics were "endowments" fixed at birth and largely determined by genetics. A series of studies from the Iowa work of Skeels and Skodak in the 1940s [published in 1949] through preschool studies of the 1960s and the even later [Carolina] Abecedarian and Infant Health and Development Program (IHDP) studies demonstrated that the potential for learning and development was not fixed at birth but was strongly influenced by environment, including parenting, the home environment, and schooling. I don't think we should back away from acknowledging that children in poverty—whose parents have less education, less money, and live in communities with weaker schools—have deficits in their environments that limit their development. Without added resources their families cannot obtain on their own they will fall behind in language, literacy, math, general cognitive development, and other domains, and these gaps will not be closed during the school years but are likely to grow larger. An appropriate response to this is enrichment.

This perspective leads away from targeted programs toward universal programs designed to meet the needs of all children. Jaqueline, your point about impoverished curricula is so important. If public programs do not offer the children who have the fewest resources at home the richest curricula, they contribute to their developmental malnourishment. I don't know how many times I have heard it said that the children "are just fine when they leave Head Start, the public schools ruin them." Yet too many aren't just fine when they leave Head Start and too many other public programs, because these programs did not give them the rich intellectual nourishment they needed to keep up with their higher-income peers and fulfill their potential.

George W. Bush spoke to the NAACP in 2006 about the "soft bigotry of low expectations." I don't find anything soft about the bigotry of low expectations. Having low expectations is a fundamental problem in both ECE and the public schools because too often ECE programs don't even try to give many children what they need to succeed at the levels they are fully capable of reaching. Leadership has a key role to play in articulating high expectations. We would do well to support increased resources together with high expectations in both home and out-of-home environments for young children and to coordinate these. To reinforce a point I made earlier, increased tax credits for families with young children, parenting support programs, and increased funding per child for nonparental ECE should not be thought of as alternatives. Programs for parents like Reach Out and Read (ROR) could be linked with child care and preschool education programs to sustain support for parental engagement begun with ROR. Such programs also can be universal.

JACQUELINE: There is no argument that disinvestment and disenfranchisement have devastated many communities, leading to conditions that seriously hinder young children from reaching their full potential. I worry that the devastation will take the foreground, and we will lose an appreciation of the humanity of the real people in those communities who get up every morning and try to make it through the day in the context of their environments. You are right that high expectations and resources are critical. I believe the explicit bias and implicit bias in education feed on diminishing the humanity of children, families, and communities, leading to a justification for lowered expectations and continuing the cycle of disinvestment and disenfranchisement. We cannot let the children be personally defined by their circumstances. And that's where high-quality early learning can be a powerful intervention, especially when followed by a strong K–12 program.

The culture wars are with us. The challenge, as I see it, is to understand the threats to the field and design a strategy that allows us to mitigate those threats while promoting equity, dignity, and self-worth for all children. There may be times when articulating our core values is the necessary and right thing to do. In such cases we must be prepared for the pushback and ready to stand our ground.

HOW HAVE CHANGES IN ECE SYSTEMS AFFECTED CLASSROOM PRACTICES WITH YOUNG CHILDREN AND THEIR FAMILIES, FOR BETTER AND/OR WORSE?

STEVE: The field has begun to devote more attention to how changes in ECE systems should affect classroom practices. Jacqueline, you highlighted two aspects of this in the previous section that have been brought into focus as some states have developed universal preschool programs. California's transformation of Transitional Kindergarten (TK) could be a pivotal moment for the field in our nation, given the state's size and the attention the state has given to planning what should happen to curriculum in preschool (formerly TK) and K–12 now that nearly all children will have attended a state-funded preschool program. This can be, to use your words, Jaqueline, a "powerful intervention" with high expectations for all children. It also presents the need and opportunity to revise K–12 practices.

To take another example from our state of New Jersey, the urban districts that made the most of providing high-quality preschool for 2 years beginning at age 3 started modifying kindergarten right away, changed early literacy instruction through grade 3, and eventually moved Algebra I down from 9th grade to 7th grade, where it typically is in the wealthier suburban districts. In California (and New Jersey, I hope someday) dual-language immersion for all children begins in preschool and continues up through grade 12.

Despite the changes we observe in policy and systems, much of the field seems focused on the debates of the past. Many seem to think that there has been a big shift from free play to direct instruction in ECE programs due to "standardization" by public programs. This is based on a romantic and inaccurate view of the past and other misconceptions. Among these is the belief that public programs, especially the public schools, are less developmentally appropriate and play-based than private programs. Yet the exact opposite is true. Private programs are more strongly didactic and have more inappropriate practices than the public schools and Head Start, though the dominant philosophy in all types of preschool programs remains DAP and play. Much more common is that practice is inconsistent and that adults have children spend much of their time waiting and in transitions, and otherwise unengaged in any activity. Classrooms can be dull and uninspiring even when children are free to play, and they can even be glued to the tube. The adults with responsibility for their care and education often have neither the preparation nor the supports needed to provide strong, positive interactions with the children. What happens in the kindergarten and early grades may be quite different from what happens in earlier ECE, though I would worry that much time may be wasted in waiting and transitions there as well. The field has been increasingly concerned that a disconnect between preschool and the early grades may erode the benefits from programs in the first 5 years of life. While this is far from certain, it is reasonable for the field to be concerned about inappropriate curriculum and pedagogy in the early grades.

JACQUELINE: We have seen state and federal regulations have a direct impact on classroom practice. For example, when the state or federal government requires a specific assessment to be used to monitor classroom quality, the teacher's practice often reflects what would be required to achieve a high score on the assessment. This can be a positive outcome, but it can also have the potential to limit the range of experiences that can enhance early learning. I have seen teachers and policymakers gain a greater interest in research that's relevant to their lives.

Perhaps more researchers are interested in the ways in which their work can have an impact on practice. There is growing interest in developing Research Practice Partnerships (RPP) in early education. The last issue of the *Future of Children* journal featured work being conducted across the country, including New York City, Boston, and Connecticut. These are long-term and mutually beneficial relationships that use research to answer real-world questions of policy and practice. I am heartened to see states, cities, and school districts willing to engage with researchers to enhance the quality of instructional practices in their ECE programs. I'm also delighted to see researchers willing to use their research skills to support the work of policymakers and practitioners. This type of work calls for a fundamental shift in the way research is typically conducted, but it has enormous potential to result in real-world evidence that can lead to continuous quality improvement.

STEVE: Some influences of changes in federal and state policy may have been more positive. For example, every state has developed strong early learning standards that approach learning and development from whole-child and developmentally appropriate perspectives. I am unsure how much they incorporate high expectations, but my impression is that classroom practice would be very much improved if these standards were taken seriously. Unfortunately, I think that all too often they don't really connect to actual practice, as there has been no serious effort to provide professional development to teachers that would help them to understand the standards and what they mean for practice or to provide the resources needed to support them in the classroom. New Jersey's Abbott program has been an exception to that pattern [see nieer.org]. The state's expectations for learning and teaching were developed with broad input from stakeholders and then supported by professional development and aligned tools for self-assessment at multiple levels in the system starting with the individual teacher and classroom. As another example, the federal government has sought to improve teacher qualifications and compensation in Head Start.

To return to an earlier point, the emphasis of means-tested federal and state programs together with other policies leaves about half of all 3- and 4-year-olds, including about half of those in poverty, not attending any ECE program at all. One recent study found that even for those in public school programs, average effect on 4th-grade achievement was close to zero. Even acknowledging that increased achievement isn't everything and is not even a necessary precursor for improved educational attainment, this should be worrying given the levels of proficiency in reading, math, and science in much of the United States. After a half-century of investing in "compensatory" ECE programs, we need a new approach, but this is not simply saying we will have "universal" programs. Too often we have found with state programs that "universal" does not mean that all children are served, nor that all children are served equally well. Of course, the solution to this need not be to revert to the failed means-tested programs of the past, but to push for universal programs to be truly universal.

WHAT INNOVATIONS ARE NEEDED FOR ECE SYSTEMS IN THE FUTURE?

STEVE: A broad universal approach that involves supports for parenting (a diverse set of policies that could include increased child tax credits for young children, parental leave, home visiting), and public programs offering everyone high-quality early care and education beginning at age 3. Between 12 and 36 months I am less clear about what is the right mix of supports. For the first year at least, it might make sense to provide stronger financial and other supports for parents to provide ECE. As the United States grows older and we become more concerned with low fertility rates, we probably should give more thought to how to make parenting more intrinsically rewarding as well as less financially burdensome.

JACQUELINE: I'm not sure the word "innovations" is the right term here for me. We already know a good deal about what works. We still need the *will* to implement these programs and policies with fidelity. I think of the often-quoted response from Larry Schweinhart, president emeritus of the HighScope Educational Research Foundation, when asked how current programs can achieve that same strength of effects as those of the Perry Preschool project. He replies, "If you want to get what we got, you need to do what we did." I would like the field to think more carefully about the components of ECE programs and which of those components have proven effective for specific subgroups of children. It might be innovative to think deeply and with communities about what program implementation might look like and identify the benefits as well as potential negative consequences. What systems need to align to create a successful program? We know what high-quality programs look like. Yet we continue to be shocked and dismayed when children don't thrive and get strong outcomes from programs that are poorly designed and lack components that have been proven to be effective.

I think ECE systems should be undergirded by a coherent birth-to-8 framework that ensures a rich set of experiences designed to foster development. We need clarity about what we're doing and why we're doing it. Perhaps broaden our goal of raising children who can just get high test scores to a national commitment to nurture children to become healthy, curious, creative, and responsible adults, children who will grow into adults who understand, respect, and can fully participate in a democratic society.

I agree, Steve, that we need a broad universal approach, and *A Roadmap to Reducing Child Poverty* [2019] reviews the impact of expanding the Earned Income Tax Credit (EITC) and the availability of the Child and Dependent Care Tax Credit (CDCTC), as well as expansion of Supplemental Nutrition Assistance Program (SNAP), housing subsidies, and minimum wage increases. Policy packages that have potential to cut child poverty by half within 10 years are identified in the report. Interestingly, the cost of these policy recommendations is argued to be less than the estimated cost of child poverty to the country. So we know what to do here also.

I would also love to see innovations in the preparation of ECE professionals. Based on a clear set of competencies, preparation programs would include both theory and practice. And a critical component would be the understanding of and capacity to build strong partnerships with parents and communities, such as those outlined in the [2015] Transforming the Workforce for Children Birth Through Age 8 report.

I've argued for some time that ECE programs need greater coordination and alignment at the federal level. Innovation might take the form of greater alignment across the major federal ECE-related funding streams such as child care, the Individuals with Disabilities Education Act (IDEA), Head Start, and Title I, and greater flexibility with state programs to facilitate implementation of mixed delivery systems. Breaking the status quo could include funding more pilot programs that examine strategies to coordinate funding, eliminating disparities in professional compensation across ECE settings, coordinating a high-level set of requitements for professional preparation, and providing financial and other supports. We might also consider funding programs at a level that can achieve high quality. The [2018] *Transforming the Financing of Early Care and Education* report is a useful starting point for understanding the cost of quality.

Furthermore, we might be better able to recruit and retain strong ECE professionals if we forgive student loans for ECE teachers who are not paid at parity with public school teachers, and actively recruit teacher preparation candidates and certified teachers who reflect the diversity of school districts.

STEVE: Jacqueline, you started at exactly the right place to think about designing ECE systems for the future. What are our goals for ECE systems? Why do we want to pursue those goals? These questions move us beyond developmental and education science to consider the moral purposes of ECE, which are both intrinsic and instrumental. Of course, then we have to move on to developmental science to inform policy and practice regarding the best ways to achieve those goals. As I think about the broad domains, I don't come up with any surprises. Within a whole-child perspective, I might emphasize empathy within the social and emotional domain because it so often seems lacking (though maybe that is just a reaction to media coverage), creativity—which we all think is important but have difficulty operationalizing and measuring—and math, because the United States does so much worse by world standards in math than in language, literacy, and even science.

Perhaps less obvious is the need for increased attention to health in ECE. The United States compares poorly on health and mortality to most other high-income countries, and the pandemic and other recent trends have reduced life spans in the United States. If we designed ECE programs to be more supportive of health, what would that mean? There are multiple pathways through which ECE supports health—directly through health screenings and connections to health services, as well as providing healthy environments, nutrition, and exercise; helping to generate lifelong dispositions and habits regarding food and activity choices; helping with stress reduction by providing less stressful environments; and improving children's capacities to prevent and reduce stress, including stronger social and emotional capacities and executive functions. Taking a very long view, improving their educational attainment has a causal impact on later-life health and mortality. That this is quite a long list for just one goal, despite being incomplete, gives a sense of the difficulty of the design task that begins with goal-setting.

Finally, approaching innovation from another perspective, we need to make major changes to the way we think about evidence-based practice. The conventional model has been to conduct rigorous studies—particularly, randomized trials—to test different policies, approaches, program standards, or practices and then to specify how the models tested should be implemented with fidelity to replicate success. Education is not a good fit for this type of approach because of the complexity of policy and practice. Individual policies, standards, and practices are not independent but interdependent. What works depends on who is being served in what contexts (thinking about Bronfenbrenner's concentric circles, this can become mind-boggling). To the extent that the "right" practices are highly idiosyncratic and change with time, a different approach to research is needed. One such approach has been recommended that generates practice-based evidence for continuous improvement to both guide local implementation and develop more broadly useful knowledge that is shared through networks. This seems more likely to take us where we want to go. However, there are major practical difficulties that take us back to some of the issues you raised—basing the preparation and compensation of teachers and leaders on our goals and what we want them to do, and designing ECE systems that have the capacities to support systems continuous improvement.

JACQUELINE: Steve, I agree strongly that we need to take a new look at how we engage in research on ECE programs. You're right to highlight the interdependence of policies, standards, and practices, the role of context. The Foundation for Child Development's [2020] publication *Getting It Right: Using Implementation Research to Improve Outcomes in Early Care and Education* is an attempt to initiate a conversation about the role of context in research to advocate for a deeper appreciation of who is being served in ECE programs.

Steve, thanks for this opportunity to reflect on the past and look to the future. It's always a pleasure talking with you. This was fun!

STEVE: Jacqueline, thank you for sharing your reflections from such a broad range of experience with science and policy. I hope readers enjoy this as much as I have!

Reflections on the Systems of Early Care and Education Conversation

Nancy E. Barbour

The big question readers may have brought to this chapter was: Is there a unified system of early childhood services in the United States? Steve and Jacqueline have tackled this difficult question using their respective knowledge and experiences to take us into an enlightening dialogue.

Steve and Jacqueline bring different, yet complementary backgrounds and perspectives to their discussion. Steve offers a macro view as an economist who has focused on early childhood programs and services. Jacqueline has a more micro view as an early childhood researcher who has interacted at the classroom and school system levels through the state and national policy levels. Both acknowledge the value of an ecological perspective à la Bronfenbrenner (1979) in thinking through ECE systems as well as the potential messiness of applying this perspective to defining ECE systems. However, both of our authors long for workable systems, as Jacqueline describes: "that help all children reach their full potential and buffer all children against the harmful consequences of poverty, racism, prejudice, and discrimination."

On the way to examining the big question, perhaps a bit of historical context is in order as we consider this discussion of early childhood systems. At the beginning of the 20th century, researchers were beginning to document how children develop and learn. The National Society for the Study of Education (NSSE) published a yearbook in 1929 that documented existing early childhood programs and the accompanying research. The programs focused on school preparation, child development, health, and parenting. The yearbook demonstrated the primacy of these early childhood programs and the impact they might have. Though an effort to establish a unifying system was not clearly stated, this documentation may have planted the seeds of an early childhood system in the United States.

With the war on poverty in the 1960s, children became a focus for intervention. Taking the position that one way to address poverty was to provide educational intervention in children's lives to compensate for the educational deficits they were experiencing, Head Start was born. Though in retrospect we see it as a deficit model, this was/is a nationally funded early childhood program. It had the potential for growing into an early childhood system, but it has not realized this larger goal in its almost 60-year history. In 1971, the Comprehensive Child Development Act was passed by Congress, but vetoed by President Nixon. This would have provided for a national child care system and national regulations governing it. There was strong objection from the anti-welfare and anti-feminist groups (see the link in the "For Further Reading" section). So close, but not to be.

As we come back to the present day, we see that the questions shift as the authors try to wrestle with the notion of what an early childhood system would be. Both Jacqueline and Steve start by defining what we would have to call nonsystems, or systems in conflict. Both note that this description is not new but has been true for many years. Steve sees these as self-organized systems or nonsystems at times, but in no way deliberate or intentional on a large scale. Jacqueline's early work as a classroom researcher urged her to view a system that went beyond the classroom, that included families, neighborhoods, and so on. Later, her work took her into school systems, where she noted the conundrum created by conflicting local and state policies. Moving on to a state system (New Jersey) and then a federal system in her work in the United States Department of Education, she clarified her understanding of the conflicting systems and funding streams at work. Educational goals were not jiving, departmental structures were in conflict, and funding streams were separate. Steve dubs this policy "incoherence." We are left to wonder, given the state of things, is it possible to have a cohesive, productive EC system? Is there common ground for considering who has access, and whether the system is one of quality?

Policy incoherence is a critical component of this dialogue. Jacqueline points out the disjunction in the school systems between values, emphases, and strategies used in preschool classrooms and the K–12 curriculum as one such incoherence. She also recounts a story of a school administrator trying to serve Head Start children in regular classrooms and confronting the inability to combine funding streams. The silos created by the divergent funding streams, the different policy bodies, and the autonomy of states to regulate early care and education make a cohesive, national ECE system seem almost impossible.

The authors identify external forces affecting an early childhood system that are cultural, economic, and political. Women entering the workforce at greater rates have certainly influenced the need for extrafamilial care arrangements. However, we have not seen efforts from the workforce to address this issue on a national scale either in terms of policy or financial support. In fact, the movement toward universal preschool programs has not, according to Steve, increased the number of young children served overall.

Politically, the efforts to make policy regarding young children remain at the state level and vary from state to state for both the development of early learning standards and child care regulation. And politics will continue to lean toward family rights and government keeping its hands off. Historically, we saw the failure of national attempts to create a national early childhood system. Steve and Jacqueline do point to pockets of good work in developing small systems of positive practice in early childhood programs such as Promise Neighborhoods.

Culture wars occasionally collide with political wars when it comes to early childhood. Steve and Jaqueline delivered their chapter after the action taken by the Alabama governor to ban the DAP book. They weigh in on the unfortunate collision of good intentions and misunderstood purpose. The political act of early childhood policy, according to Steve and Jacqueline, puts all of early childhood education, and particularly NAEYC, as the professional association, on alert and ready to withstand the interrogation of their work. This seems like one more deterrent to a cohesive early childhood system.

Perhaps the most pervasive system that has emerged over time is the system of testing of young children, focusing on academic skills as a means of measuring success of programs, children, and teachers. Though this has been mostly a state-regulated system, it has narrowly defined both the purpose and value of early childhood programs. However, this testing system has defined school success as well as teacher competence. It is a system that lacks the focus that Jacqueline so clearly defined in the statement about desired early childhood programs. However, she and Steve see the value of a different approach, Research Practice Partnerships. This approach supports research that provides a continuous feedback loop to improve practice, policy, and systems and is being used in several different states.

Where does this leave us in understanding the state of our early childhood system? Is it possible in a country so diverse to have a clearly defined system? Is it a desirable aim? What would it look like? Jacqueline and Steve speculated on what such a system might be. Steve discussed a system that provided true universal access for children and families, not just "universal" for some. These programs would provide economic support for parents with benefits such as tax credits, paid family leave, and support for families both educationally and financially. Most of all, the programs would be of high quality and taught by qualified, well-compensated educational professionals. Jacqueline was specific about needing an early childhood system that covered children from birth to age 8 that consists of the elements that we already know are working, relying on the extant research and recommendations from documents like *Transforming the Workforce* and *A Roadmap to Reducing Child Poverty*. She would hope to see better alignment between preschool educational practices and kindergarten-through-12th-grade practices. Would that it be so.

QUESTIONS FOR DISCUSSION

1. Is it possible or desirable to have a national early childhood system?
2. How might we shift public will toward supporting early childhood systems?
3. What is your vision of an ideal early childhood system?

FOR FURTHER READING

Barnett, W. S., & Frede, E. C. (2017). Long-term effects of a system of high-quality universal preschool education in the United States (pp. 152–172). In H. P. Blossfeld, N. Kulic, J. Skopek, & M. Triventi (Eds), *Childcare, early education and social inequality: An international perspective*. Edward Elgar Publishing.

Bronfenbrenner, U. (1979). *The ecology of human development: Experiments by nature and design*. Harvard University Press.

Institute of Medicine (IOM) and National Research Council (NRC). (2015). Transforming the workforce for children birth through 8: A unifying foundation. The National Academies Press.

Jones, J. (2023). Toward transforming fragmented and unequal early years systems—recommendations. In M. Nagasawa, L. Peters, M. N. Bloch, & B. B. Swadener, *Transforming early years policy in the U.S.: A call to action* (pp. 25–30). Teachers College Press.

National Academies of Sciences, Engineering, and Medicine (2019). *A roadmap to reducing child poverty*. The National Academies Press.

1971 Comprehensive Child Development Act link: https://www.congress.gov/bill/93rd-congress/house-bill/1083#:~:text=Comprehensive%20Child%20Development%20Act%20%2D%20States,greatest%20economic%20and%20social%20needs

CHAPTER 2

Diversity, Equity, and Children's Rights in Early Childhood Education

Gloria Swindler Boutte and Dina C. Castro

Dr. Gloria Swindler Boutte is an associate dean of Diversity, Equity, and Inclusion and a Carolina Distinguished Professor at the University of South Carolina. Her scholarship focuses on equity pedagogies. She is the author/editor of seven books: *Revolutionary Love for Early Childhood Classrooms: Nurturing the Brilliance of Young Black Children; Educating African American Students: And How Are the Children? (2nd edition)*; *We Be Lovin' Black Children: Learning to Be Literate About the African Diaspora* (2022 Society of Professors of Education Outstanding Book Award); *African Diaspora Literacy: The Heart of Transformation in K–12 Schools and Teacher Education* (2019 AESA Critics Choice Award); *Resounding Voices: School Experiences of People From Diverse Ethnic Backgrounds;* and *Multicultural Education: Raising Consciousness*. She has served as a visiting scholar and presented her work internationally on every continent except for Antarctica.

Dr. Dina C. Castro is the Bahamdan Endowed Professor in Early Childhood Well-Being and Director of the Institute for Early Childhood Well-Being at Wheelock College of Education & Human Development, Boston University. Her scholarship focuses on equity and quality in the early education of bilingual children in immigrant and indigenous communities in the United States and Latin America. She has published two books: *New Voices ~ Nuevas Voces: Guide to Cultural and Linguistic Diversity in Early Childhood* (first author) and *Language, Learning and Disability in the Education of Young Bilingual Children* (co-editor and author), and has over 70 publications including journal articles, book chapters, and research and policy reports. Dr. Castro has served as visiting professor and graduate faculty through research collaborations with academic institutions in Africa, Europe and Latin America. She is a Fulbright Specialist and a representative of the World Organization for the Education of Young Children at the United Nations.

GLORIA & DINA: We love the larger concept of this book—looking back and looking forward. It reminds us of an African principle, *sankofa*. The term *sankofa* is from the Akan people of Ghana (West Africa) and translates to "go back and get it," which connotes that both the past and future are important. We also note at the onset that though this chapter focuses on equity and diversity, we believe that diversity should also be integrated throughout *all* topics in this book.

Because of the nature of the topic (equity and diversity), we wanted it to be particularly dialogic. We also knew that it was important for us to organically draw from our cultural communication styles. In our prewriting discussion, we found common cultural themes and communication styles that we will embed in this chapter. For example, both of our cultural backgrounds (African American and Latine) routinely use narratives. Therefore, we embed stories and vignettes in our responses when possible. We also jointly respond to some of the questions rather than individually for a few reasons. First, both of our cultural frameworks are communal (versus individualistic). From this perspective, our conversations are typically inclusive of others. Our conversations tend to be interactional rather than sequential (circular rather than linear). Second, African American Language (AAL) speakers routinely communicate using *call and response* (one person speaks and then expects the other person or the audience to respond in some way)—e.g., *Are you with me?* (Yes!); *Holla back!* (Amen!). Third, African American Language and Spanish speakers use *overlapping* and *co-narration* during which more than one person can speak or two or more people tag-team telling the story.

AS YOU ENTERED YOUR CAREER, WHAT WERE THE COMMON UNDERSTANDINGS/POSITIONS ABOUT DIVERSITY AND CHILDREN'S RIGHTS?

GLORIA: I entered my career in 1980 as a teacher, and later a Child Development Specialist. In general, diversity issues were peripheral and superficial. The dominant theories, research, and teaching strategies were (and still are) Eurocentric, though often presented as universal. At the same time, NAEYC demonstrated awareness of the need to include representation of children from diverse racial, ethnic, and cultural backgrounds on the cover of the *Young Children* journal—which was not a popular thing to do at the time. This imagery appealed to me and made a strong symbolic statement about valuing diversity. I often saved the covers of the journal as artwork. NAEYC's conferences intentionally featured Black scholars of color like Janice Hale and Carol Brunson.

DINA: I also entered the field in the early 1980s. I was first a psychology intern and then obtained my license as a clinical psychologist. This was in Lima, Peru. Working as a psychologist at a health center in a low-income community, I learned that children attending local schools were repeating 1st grade up to three times because they were not learning to read and write. I decided to put my efforts into supporting early childhood programs.

In the early 1990s, I emigrated to the United States, where I continued my journey in the field of early childhood care and education. In both countries, the dominant theories and research informing early education policies and teaching practices were (and I agree, they still are) Eurocentric. For example, instruments to assess young children's development in Peru were translations (without cultural validity) of instruments designed in the United States or European countries. In the United States, child development assessments developed based on the characteristics and experiences of white, middle-class, monolingual English-speaking children were used with children from diverse racial, cultural, and linguistic backgrounds. Furthermore, children growing up bilingually were assessed only in English, a practice that is still prevalent in most early childhood programs and schools around the country after 30 years.

GLORIA: I was onboard and active with NAEYC when the first DAP position statement was just a working draft of a position statement that was being circulated in ECE circles nationwide. It was an exciting and hopeful time, though, in the early 1990s as I continued to deepen my own knowledge base on equity and diversity, I could readily identify the need for culturally appropriate practices. I began to understand systemic and structural issues and the need for voices of people of color to be included in ECE leadership decisions, in policies, publications, and so forth. I came to understand how inequities are endemic in ECE curriculum, instruction, policies, and assessments.

Importantly, I understood that culture cannot simply be an add-on when developing policies and curriculum.

A comparison of my earlier and current scholarship will make it apparent that my scholarship and teaching have become increasingly more critical over the decades. Three key works (among others) helped me rethink superficially cultural foci: Paulo Freire's *Pedagogy of the Oppressed* [2018], Herbert Kohl's *Should We Burn Babar* [1996], and Bruce Mallory and Rebecca New's *Diversity and Developmentally Appropriate Practices* [1994]. I also engaged ECE preservice and inservice teachers around some of the robust discussions that probed DAP and urged the dynamic development of the construct. We delved into writings by Gaile Canella, Daniel Walsh, Rebecca New, Sue Bredekamp, and others to better understand different dimensions of DAP and what was or was not missing. Organizations like Reconceptualizing Early Childhood Education (RECE) have led the way on some of the decolonizing pedagogies, though I still hold that the racial piece still needs development.

DINA: In the 1970s and 1980s in Latin America, the works of Paulo Freire were very influential, in particular, given the social and political circumstances our countries were going through. The transformational role of education as a field that could help to build a democratic society, where human and, specifically, children's rights would be respected, were at the core of Freire's thoughts. Freire's critical pedagogy guided my work and helped me explain the contradictions and absences I found in early education research, policies, and practices, and to think about how to contribute to change that.

Early in my career I learned about inequities that resulted from poverty and exclusion, and how they affected young children's development and learning. Moving to the United States, I found similarities between the experiences of young children from low-income circumstances in both countries. Essentially, the social mechanisms were the same. Poverty affected mostly children from racial, ethnic, and language minoritized communities. I added to my previous knowledge the ecological theory of child development proposed by Bronfenbrenner that considered contextual factors in the lives of children, and not only their individual characteristics. However, it did not explicitly identify the roles of structural racism and discrimination in children's experiences. In the late 1990s, Cynthia Garcia-Coll, a Latina researcher, and her colleagues proposed a conceptual model to understand development of children in minoritized communities, and later, more specifically, of children in immigrant families. What is still missing in the work of child development scholars is the focus on the early years of life and the experiences of young children from racially and linguistically minoritized communities.

From the perspective of early childhood education, DAP appeared to address some of the questions about the diverse experiences of young children. It evolved over the years to give consideration to culture, race, language, and ability in the early education of young children. I was active with NAEYC during the latest revision of DAP that occurred when NAEYC was also preparing a position statement on advancing equity in early childhood education.

Throughout my professional work, I have been engaged in research and teacher preparation to promote early childhood practices that take into account children's bilingualism in contexts where their first or native language has been minoritized. Although progress has been made to acknowledge and promote equity and diversity in early childhood education, language diversity and linguistic discrimination have not been sufficiently addressed in early childhood research and practice. Theoretical perspectives on language racialization and linguistic racism from the emergent field of raciolinguistics proposed by Rosa and Flores, Dovchin, and Alim, among others, can help explain how language is used to perpetuate the marginalization of communities of color. This is evident when analyzing language policies and practices in early childhood programs that ignore minoritized children's diverse linguistic abilities. They immerse children in English-only education, leading to the loss of their other language.

WHERE HAS THE UNITED STATES STOOD IN COMPARISON TO OTHER COUNTRIES REGARDING RESPONSES TO DIVERSITY AND CONSIDERATION OF THE RIGHTS OF CHILDREN? HOW HAS THAT IMPACTED ECE PRACTICE?

DINA: Considering that each country has its own social, cultural, and demographic characteristics, it is difficult to make comparisons that could be meaningful. However, there might be aspects that could provide some food for thought and from which we could learn. The closest reference I have for a comparison is my experience in Latin America. I will answer this question focusing on language policies, linguistic rights, and language(s) use in education.

A Peruvian poet said about the diversity of Peru: *"No, no hay país más diverso, más múltiple en variedad terrena y humana; todos los grados de calor y color, de amor y odio, de urdimbres y sutilezas, de símbolos utilizados e inspiradores . . ."* ["No, there is no country more diverse, more multiple in terrestrial and human variety; all degrees of heat and color, of love and hate, of warps and subtleties, of used and inspiring symbols . . ."] (José María Arguedas). The diversity of Peru also exists in other countries in the Latin American region, where there are over 500 indigenous communities and 23% of the population is of African descent. Educational and language policies to address these diversities vary across countries, but many have policies that explicitly intend to combat exclusion and provide educational opportunities that respect and incorporate indigenous and Afro descendants' cultures and languages. The challenges are in the implementation of those policies. In Peru, for example, by law all indigenous languages in the country (47 in 2023) are official languages along with Spanish, the language of the colonizer, and the country's dominant language. Giving official status to indigenous languages meant an increased budget allocation by the government for intercultural bilingual education (IBE) offered to indigenous children in their communities. Generally, migrants from these communities in urban areas do not have access to IBE, although, there are plans to implement an Intercultural Education for All initiative (not bilingual) in urban areas. Also, efforts were made to create writing for oral indigenous languages in order to develop textbooks.

Thinking about language diversity and language policies in the United States, according to the U.S. Census Bureau, there are over 350 languages spoken by families in the country, including those spoken by children in Native nations and children of immigrants. Currently, about one in five people in the United States speak a language other than English. This is without considering speakers of African American Language and dialectal variations of English spoken by other minoritized communities around the country. In spite of this growing diversity, language policies over the years have been assimilationist and segregationist, with no or little support for the right of children from racially and ethnically minoritized communities to maintain and develop their native languages and cultures. "The ideology that English is the default 'norm' in the United States is steeped in a colonial and racialized history" (Castro & Meek, 2022). Bilingual education programs were designed for English language acquisition, and not with the goal of children becoming proficient in both their native language and English. Moreover, children having abilities in a language other than English was (and still is) seen as a "language barrier." Change has been slow and not very significant. At the time we are writing this chapter, about 80% of the children speaking a language other than English are placed in English as a Second Language programs (with no support for bilingualism), and only about 20% have access to dual-language education, a bilingual education model that supports bilingual development and learning. Furthermore, bilingual education programs are available in very few languages and target the needs of K–12 students. Most bilingual education policies have not included the early childhood education of young bilingual children. The Head Start program has the most robust standards specific to educating young bilingual children, which include teaching practices to support development of children's language other than English and hiring bilingual staff, among others.

The advantages of bilingualism have been demonstrated for years; research and scientific evidence should have informed policies in support of bilingualism and biliteracy. However, a double standard exists by which becoming bilingual or multilingual is still seen as a barrier for racially and ethnically minoritized populations, and as an enrichment opportunity for white middle-class English-speaking children whose families are increasingly requesting access to dual-language education for their children. Progress toward equity in early childhood education has been made, but there is a long way to go to reach that goal.

GLORIA: Given that the United States is more culturally diverse than many countries, comparisons are complicated. At the same time, since we are all globally interconnected (*ubuntu,*—a South African term that means "I am because we are"), it is a fair question.

Before responding to this question, let me just acknowledge that biliteracy and bilingualism among African American Language speakers are typically overlooked in the literature. I have written about this several times over the years. Now, back to the question.

One of the first things that came to my mind when thinking about diversity and children's rights was Reggio Emilia. Reading about the 100 languages of children and other aspects of Reggio—and later having a chance to visit on a study tour, in 1999—I was fascinated by the respect for children's "languages" and the myriad of ways of expressing themselves. Likewise, the co-construction of knowledge among the children and adults made sense to me and was familiar to me culturally. Yet, because most of the children in the programs at the time (I have not kept up with it) were Italian, racial identities were not a part of the equation. As my professional and personal lives center Black culture and experiences, over time, I was still yearning for more. I still think Reggio's respect for young children is amazing. I would love a world in which Black children were respected and in which their cultures were centered. In a racially stratified society like the United States, children's racial identities play a key role in their development in ways beyond how we typically consider social and emotional development.

In the early 2000s, I had the honor of working with early childhood educators like Glenda McNaughton in Australia, whose work on children's rights was amazing. More recently, Australian scholars like Helen Adam are also doing important work around equity in children's literature and also tackling anti-Blackness (a worldwide phenomenon).

WHAT HAVE BEEN THE SUCCESSES, DEAD ENDS, AND/OR FAILURES IN ADDRESSING DIVERSITY IN ECE PRACTICE?

GLORIA: Successes include NAEYC and other professional organizations trying to incorporate culturally appropriate practices into the DAP construct. Yet the field has much work to do. In ECE settings and teacher preparation programs, we have not integrated a deep understanding of culture. We still rely heavily on white theories, research methodologies, and practices. Children's literature in classrooms rarely includes the worldviews of people of color. Discussions with young children about racial issues are often avoided, and color blindness prevails.

I think the time is ripe for the ECE field to continue, amplify, and extend an unapologetic commitment to dismantling anti-Black racism and other forms of racism, sexism, ableism, heterosexism, and so forth. A key part of working toward equity is for ECE educators to begin by doing deep archeological digs (nod to Yolanda Seily-Ruiz) into our respective and multiple social identities. Likewise, we have to begin to understand diversity, equity, and inclusion beyond the level of the individual child and learn about how systemic inequities in curriculum, instruction, policies, and assessment manifest themselves—and what we can do about it.

DINA: I definitely concur with the points you mention, Gloria. From my perspective, the conversations about equity and diversity in the field have changed from identifying the need for and incorporating culturally appropriate, and then culturally *and* linguistically appropriate practices to identifying the need for and proposing culturally sustaining and antiracist pedagogical approaches, going deeper into the roots of the persistent inequities in the education of young children. This is reflected in the evolution of NAEYC's position statements. Along with revising DAP, in 2019 NAEYC published its position statement on *Advancing Equity in Early Childhood Education*. As a member of the board, I had the honor to be part of the committee that elaborated on the document. The statement recognizes children's right to equitable learning opportunities, and structural racism, classism, ableism, sexism, and other structural societal barriers. Also, it states that early educators have a professional obligation to embrace diversity and inclusion and work to eliminate structural inequities affecting children's educational opportunity. This has definitely been an important step forward for the ECE field.

It has taken 2 decades to get to this point, but finally we have arrived at a time in which we can be open and unapologetic about defending children's rights. What I mean is that the discourse as a field has changed, and that the hard work in generating the scientific knowledge that supports it and the advocacy of many of us, practitioners and researchers, over the years has paved the road to reach this point.

WHAT EFFORTS ARE NEEDED IN THE FUTURE TO ENSURE THAT CLASSROOM PRACTICES VALUE DIVERSITY AND PROTECT CHILDREN'S RIGHTS?

DINA: Classroom practices are the reflection of program/school policies, and those are linked to state and national ECE policies. There is more work to do at the policy level to ensure that accountability systems are developed based on equity, diversity, and inclusion principles. We need to go beyond the "add-on" approach that is used in curricula, teacher preparation, and research by adding a "multicultural" module, lesson, or research sample, while maintaining a predominantly white, middle-class, monolingual, heterosexual, and "typically developing child" approach.

Early educators' beliefs and dispositions, not only their knowledge, influence their teaching practices. Early educators' implicit and explicit biases should be addressed in teacher preparation and professional development, giving them the tools (e.g., teaching strategies, materials, ongoing support through coaching) they need to implement practices that promote fairness and justice in early education, offering children from minoritized communities the opportunity to flourish in the early childhood classroom and beyond.

For bilingual children, fostering linguistic freedom in the early childhood classroom is crucial, but there are still too many children attending early childhood programs only in English where teachers and program administrators actively reject children's language other than English, a language through which they learn and connect with others, the language of their emotions and their cultural heritage. Referring to that language as their "home language" is already situating an essential part of the child outside the classroom, harming children's learning, identity, and self-concept. We need to embrace children as complete human beings, with all their languages and cultures. Often teachers have said to me that parents are the ones asking them not to use their children's native language in the classroom. We need to empower families of bilingual children, giving them access to the research evidence about the benefits of bilingualism for their children's development and help them see it as an asset they have and not as a barrier or deficit.

GLORIA: As a field, we need unapologetic efforts around addressing children's racial identities, languages, and cultures. We should think about the right to deeply integrate this content and dispositions as *human rights*. Our silence and fears of political and social attacks are unacceptable. Our reification of whiteness in the ECE curriculum leaves us unwittingly complicit in racism. As I have written about, when we do not privilege the right for children's cultures, worldviews, and voices to be deeply included in ECE fields, we subject children to various types of violence (e.g., linguistic attacks on their language; symbolic attacks on their culture—often through invisibility)—though that is not our intent.

None of this is to vilify us as educators, as I believe that ECE teachers are amazing. All of this is to say that without conscious and strategic plans to center diversity, equity, and inclusion, we will do harm, thus violating the first ethical professional principle: *First, do no harm.* I am speaking from my own experiences and note that I am on an ongoing journey (one that I enjoy, by the way) to learn to teach and research in ways that honor children who have been and are minoritized. I make mistakes along the way, but that is par for the course. It does not prevent me from understanding that I have an obligation to ensure children's human rights, and this often includes going against the grain when it comes to minoritized children's needs.

Reflections on the Diversity, Equity, and Children's Rights in Early Childhood Education Conversation

Nancy File

Gloria and Dina have given us much to consider in their stories and perspectives. Before moving into that, a short explanation from the editors' viewpoint about chapter sequence. We began with an examination of the systems comprising the early childhood education field. This is akin to setting the scene regarding where and how the field meets its clients, young children, and their families. We positioned the chapter on diversity and equity next to emphasize its primacy. As Dina and Gloria detailed, those of us working today inherited *and* own a field with a longtime Eurocentric emphasis. I recall many textbooks over decades in which a chapter on "diversity" or "multiculturalism" appeared at the end of the table of contents. From today's vantage point, this can more readily be seen as an implicit message that up until that point, we must have been discussing the typical (read Eurocentric) way of doing things, with a nod to those outside this circle coming once the conversation is established. And so we want readers *from the start* to consider the many communities of children and families they will meet in their work. Early childhood programs only work for *all* children if from the foundation upward, we are aware of who each and all of those children are, what experiences they and their communities have had, and what it means for them to fulfill their potential within our walls.

At the same time, consideration of diversity and equity issues is not limited to this chapter, and readers will note other contributors discussing their own growth experiences in understanding traditional confines within the field. The topics we have divided into chapters overlap in reality. Thus, the contributors for the previous chapter referred to the Developmentally Appropriate Practice (DAP) position statement from the National Association for the Education of Young Children (NAEYC), as do Dina and Gloria in this chapter. In the next chapter, DAP is the sole focus. We urge readers to look for connections among chapters and the contributors' experiences and perspectives.

I begin the reflection on our chapter focused on diversity, equity, and children's rights with a brief journey to the 1980s, when Gloria and Dina started their careers. As Gloria and Dina shared, there have been changes, but it seems apropos to provide some examination of the starting point. I examined all of the issues of NAEYC's journal, *Young Children*, published in volume 35 (November 1979 through September 1980), and I found only four articles explicitly including groups who were not white. If minoritized groups were not mentioned, the articles concerned "children" and reflected the dominant Eurocentric assumptions. Two articles were concerned with the population group identified as Hispanic at the time. One article, "Providing Child Care for Hispanic Families," (issue 6, September 1980) discussed the need for bilingual staffing, staff training, dual-language materials, and responsiveness to culture. The second article was a review of research, "Bilingualism in Early Childhood" (issue 4, May 1980). By 1980, the research literature had established that early bilingual development did not have negative effects (it was and still is common to think it does) and may have positive effects, although there were still many questions. As an aside, the research performed in the last 40 years, as Dina noted, presents a much stronger foundation for fully supporting bilingualism and its accompanying benefits. The third article, "Early Education for Asian American Children," (issue 2, January 1980) described cultural values found in various Asian countries. Finally, a piece entitled "Reading, Writing, and Dialect" (issue 1, November 1979) took on the topic of Black English, as it was called (African American Language in the chapter). This was a reprint from a *Washington Post* newspaper columnist who argued that dialect speakers should not be approached as inferior and should be allowed to use Black English when "standard English" was not a requirement (e.g., job site).

What does this array of articles tell us? First, they illustrate the add-on nature of diversity perspectives, as Gloria described it. There was early childhood, and then there were additional considerations for particular groups. This would, in effect, render those groups invisible until they were highlighted.

Second, they illustrate debates about language (ongoing still), a topic touched upon by both Dina and Gloria. All levels of education,

ECE included, have operated with assimilationist policies forcing children to leave their first languages at the door. The operating assumptions include that being bilingual and/or bidialectal is too much for young children, not important to their lives, too difficult to support, and/or a problem that threatens English proficiency. All these beliefs ignore the vital connections between language and culture. The topic of language, so essential to personhood, remains vexed in education.

Third, the articles of that era do little to explore the meaning of cultural diversity for classroom practices serving children from a range of backgrounds. One article, the discussion of Asian cultures, put forth that there were two major schools of thought concerning cultural diversity: Should cultural practices of minoritized groups be seen as something that needs to be changed (the assimilationist/deficit perspective), or should programs change teaching in response to diversity in cultural practices (adapting to differences children bring with them)? In other words, forcing children to conform to dominant cultural practices was presented as an option with benefits and drawbacks; it was essentially presented as allowing children to find success in the dominant culture.

Finally, this selection of articles reflects the ethos of the time. Research often compared minoritized groups to white norms. Desired program goals were taken for granted while being driven by dominant values (e.g., how one should use language). There was little examination of ideology or values underlying the field's definition of good practices.

Unsurprisingly, given this brief review, Gloria recalled that she found ideology and practices pertinent to minoritized groups of children to be "peripheral and superficial" at the start of her career. Dina described responses to children who came (and still come) to programs with a first language other than English marked as having a "barrier" rather than an opportunity. These perspectives are reflected in the first edition of the DAP position statement, published in 1986. The position statement was based upon a universal perspective of human development, similar for all and decontextualized (which was the default position of research at the time). Children were described as having individual differences, in part related to "family background." What was meant by "family background" was not specified. While there was a recommendation to broaden experiences for all children based on family/cultural backgrounds and to respectfully accept differences, there was no attention given to how values, ways of being, and everyday practices are deeply embedded in societal and cultural contexts. Was "respecting" differences sufficient to provide optimal learning experiences to children?

At the same time, there were glimmers of change. In 1989, NAEYC published *Anti-Bias Curriculum: Tools for Empowering Young Children*. A later edition, *Anti-Bias Education for Young Children and Ourselves* (NAEYC, 2009), broadened the scope to include teachers. The stated purposes of the text included increasing children's comfort with differences and facilitating their ability to recognize unfairness. The second edition of the NAEYC DAP position statement in 1997 more clearly included cultural diversity, after critique of its absence from the first (1987) edition. Still, people expressed concern that culture was reflected as an add-on to the unacknowledged dominance of the Eurocentric perspective.

One influence mentioned by both Gloria and Dina was Paulo Freire's *Pedagogy of the Oppressed*. Freire has had less influence in the early childhood field compared to other levels of education. This may be because of the dominance of the research-based child development perspective within ECE. Those concerned with the philosophy of education, such as John Dewey from the United States and Paulo Freire from Brazil, infrequently appear on reading lists informed by developmental research. Freire wrote about education as a means to question and challenge domination in the social system. In his view, education could be transformative, rather than enabling ongoing decades of oppression. One of his most well-known concepts is of banking in education, that education designed to reinforce the status quo operates by filling passive learners with knowledge, similar to the concepts of the blank slate or filling the empty vessel. Here, it is deposited, or banked, within individuals who are not expected to ask questions or discuss problems, but to stay in place.

Both Dina and Gloria believe that there is still much work to be done in the area of diversity and equity (the latter concept being of more recent use). Making inroads into providing more culturally responsive or sustaining learning experiences for young children is only a part of working toward equity within the systems of early childhood. One of the principles the editors discussed among ourselves when conceiving the idea of this book was "don't be satisfied until you have troubled the waters." What arose in those discussions was the tendency of those new to the field to believe that current practices represent a pinnacle of knowledge ("here's how to do it!"), not merely the latest iteration of defining the field. By troubling the waters, looking beneath the surface, we can see more clearly what Dina termed the "contradictions and absences." Gloria and Dina examined a long road to where we are now, clarifying as well that there is a long road still in front of us. Both contributors stressed that equity issues have gained a more prominent place of discussion. Far from the starting place 4 decades ago of "respecting differences" (a viewpoint, according to Dina that did not acknowledge "structural racism and discrimination"), the field has come to new perspectives—that it cannot serve children well without acknowledging "systemic inequities" (Gloria). Thus, it was an important moment when NAEYC published a position statement on *Advancing Equity in Early Childhood Education* in 2019. This work also served as one of the foundations for the fourth edition of the DAP position statement. And yet, this work also served as the entry point for DAP to become part of today's hotly debated political climate, as described in the previous chapter.

Our questions for Dina and Gloria included reference to children's rights. Outside of the United States this is an issue commonly discussed, yet it is not front and center in the dialogue within our country. This may be in part because the United Nations Convention on the Rights of the Child, adopted in 1989, was eventually ratified by all countries *except* the United States. In other countries, discussion has been shaped around the issue of how policy and practice intersect with children's rights. In the United States, currently, discussion of rights seems more tied to issues in the Bill of Rights, such as the right to bear arms and freedom of speech.

Gloria and Dina made a call to be "unapologetic" in the work of providing culturally sustaining programs for children, addressing biases grounded in racism and other -isms and making commitments to dismantle inequitable systems and practices. Gloria made a plea to "center" diversity, equity, and inclusion efforts in our work. By tying these practices to the rights that children might/should/do possess in society, we build a foundation to ensure that all children and families are granted the dignity of their culture being accepted as vital to their personhood and given the opportunity to participate in programs that acknowledge and support their strengths and full potential.

QUESTIONS FOR DISCUSSION

1. Gloria and Dina cite the importance of digging deeply into identities, both one's own identities and the cultural/social

context of minoritized groups. What are some ways you can do this work? What supports are needed for this learning?

2. In the early childhood years, the percentage of children in programs or schools who speak a first language other than English is higher than at other levels of education. What will prepare you to work effectively with children who arrive in your classroom speaking one of the hundreds of non-English languages found in the United States? What systems are needed to support the children within the many different types of early childhood programs that exist?
3. One of the perspectives shared in this chapter is the rights of children. What do you believe should be included as rights that all children should have?

FOR FURTHER READING

Alanís, I., & Iruka, I. U., with Friedman, S. (Eds.). (2021). *Advancing equity and embracing diversity in early childhood education: Elevating voices and actions*. National Association for the Education of Young Children.

Boutte, G. S. (2022). *Educating African American students: And how are the children?* (2nd ed.). Routledge.

Boutte, G. S., Earick, M., & Jackson, T. (2021). Linguistic policies for African American Language Speakers: Moving from anti-blackness to problackness. *Theory Into Practice, 60*(3), 231–241.

Castro, D. C., & Meek, S. (2022). Beyond Castañeda and the "language barrier" ideology: Young children and their right to bilingualism. *Language Policy, 21*, 407–425.

Castro, D. C., & Prishker, N. (2019). Early childhood care and education for bilingual children and the road to multilingualism. In C. P. Brown, M. B. McMullen, & N. File (Eds.), *The Wiley handbook of early childhood care and education* (pp. 173–196). Wiley-Blackwell.

Freire, P. (2018). *Pedagogy of the oppressed 50th anniversary edition* (4th ed.). Bloomsbury.

Iruka, I. U., Durden, T. R., Escayg, K-A., & Curenton, S. M. (2023). *We are the change we seek: Advancing racial justice in early care and education.* Teachers College Press.

National Association for the Education of Young Children. (2019). *Advancing Equity in Early Childhood Education Position Statement.* https://www.naeyc.org/sites/default/files/globally-shared/downloads/PDFs/resources/position-statements/advancingequitypositionstatement.pdf

CHAPTER 3

Developmentally Appropriate Practice

The Position Statement of the National Association for the Education of Young Children

Sue Bredekamp and Marilou Hyson

Sue Bredekamp is an early education specialist who serves as a consultant on developmentally appropriate practice, curriculum, teaching, and professional development for state and national organizations and institutions of higher education. She edited NAEYC's highly influential publications on *Developmentally Appropriate Practice in Early Childhood Programs*. Employed at NAEYC for 18 years, she developed and directed their accreditation system for early learning programs and wrote numerous position statements. Sue is the author of an introductory teacher education textbook, *Effective Practices in Early Childhood Education: Building a Foundation.* Sue is co-chair of the National Academies of Sciences Committee on a New Vision for High Quality Pre-K Curriculum. She has served on numerous advisory boards, including the National Research Council's Committee on Early Childhood Mathematics. Sue has been a visiting lecturer at Macquarie University in Sydney, Australia; Monash University in Melbourne; New Zealand Tertiary College; the University of Alaska; and the University of Hawaii.

Marilou Hyson is a national and international early childhood consultant. Her work focuses on social and emotional development, early childhood interventions and policies, and teacher professional development. After receiving her Ph.D. from Bryn Mawr College, she was a faculty member and then chair of the University of Delaware's Department of Individual and Family Studies. Following her academic service, Marilou was a Society for Research in Child Development Executive Branch fellow and then, for 6 years, Associate Executive Director for Professional Development at the National Association for the Education of Young Children (NAEYC). There she guided the development of position statements and helped implement NAEYC's professional preparation standards. Internationally, Marilou has been a senior advisor to UNICEF, the World Bank, and Save the Children. In that role, she has supported low-income countries' development of teacher competency standards and professional development programs.

OVER THE COURSE OF YOUR CAREER, WHAT HAVE YOU SEEN AS SOME OF THE MAJOR INFLUENCES OF THE DAP POSITION STATEMENT, STARTING IN 1986/1987 AND WITH REVISIONS, INCLUDING THE MOST RECENT ONE?

SUE: Looking back over the last 40+ years, NAEYC's position statement on Developmentally Appropriate Practice has had a major impact on the field—for the most part, a very positive influence, but at times less so. The book was first published in 1986, an expanded edition quickly followed in 1987, and then revisions in 1997, 2009, and 2022. (The approval dates of the position statement precede the books, but we use the book dates to avoid confusion.) At each point in its evolution, the statement was used in multiple ways to improve programs for children and professional development of educators. However, various weaknesses also became evident. Fortunately, the most glaring weaknesses were criticized and debated, which contributed to significant change in subsequent revisions.

It's important to remember that DAP is a position statement of NAEYC. Typically, the Association takes a research-based position on an issue of controversy or current issues confronting the field, such as a situation that potentially affects the health and well-being of children and families or educators. DAP has been revised approximately every 10 years to reflect the current knowledge base and context, and to correct misunderstandings or misrepresentations. Development of position statements involves many steps, beginning with a diverse committee of experts, open hearings at conferences, widespread review and input by hundreds of people, and finally, approval by the elected Governing Board that scrutinizes and eventually arrives at consensus on practically every word.

Two trends led to NAEYC's initially taking a position on developmentally appropriate practice. First was the pressing need to increase understanding and interpretation of accreditation standards for the system to achieve its goal of improving the quality of programs for young children. And second was the urge to counteract the trend toward pushdown curriculum in kindergarten and preschool.

In 1985, NAEYC launched its accreditation system after 4 years of development, field testing, and the involvement of literally thousands of people. It is hard to imagine now that the final draft of the accreditation criteria was printed in *Young Children* and distributed for review and comment to the then 40,000 members. We knew from the outset that we would soon need to define *developmentally appropriate* because the term was used throughout the standards. In fact, I vividly remember being in some hotel room during the very first validation visit we ever had. A friend of mine who'd done the visit called and said, "They don't know what's developmentally appropriate." Over the 15 years when I administered accreditation, DAP definitely had a positive influence on the system, and I assume it continues to do so.

A second impetus for adopting DAP was the trend toward preschoolers being served in public schools. Early childhood educators lamented the fact that 1st-grade curriculum and teaching practices were being pushed down to kindergarten and feared that the trend would continue as increasing numbers of preschoolers attended public schools. Out of this arose the call for clarity about what is and is not appropriate for young children. Ironically and sadly, the field was very upset about this trend in 1985, but in the last 40 years the situation has only gotten worse. As for the goal of countering pushdown curriculum and teaching overall, DAP failed to have the hoped-for impact, particularly regarding kindergarten. NAEYC defines early childhood as birth through age 8, and DAP covered that full age span from the beginning. The "Green Book," as it came to be known, connected NAEYC to primary grades for the first time, although it has never had the impact in kindergarten and the early grades that was envisioned.

So, what has been DAP's major impact and influence? My personal opinion has always been that the Governing Board's decision to include examples of both appropriate and inappropriate practices was the reason for DAP's immediate and lasting impact on the field. Prior to that, we had stated everything in positive terms (except "staff refrain from corporal punishment" in accreditation criteria). Without those two columns contrasting appropriate with inappropriate, I believe that DAP would have been just another early childhood book on a shelf. By including the columns, we inadvertently ensured that the book would not only be noticed but used, because it was significantly different from every other early childhood text. In fact, the 1987 DAP book was almost evangelically embraced by the field, selling more than 700,000 copies.

At the same time, the column format created significant problems and misinterpretations by oversimplifying the complex role of the teacher. There were numerous other flaws in the 1987 document, to be discussed in Question 2.

MARILOU: Sue, I'm not sure I would call myself evangelical, but like many others in the field, during those early years I had experiences that created a readiness for what the DAP position and resources offered. While you were laboring away at NAEYC headquarters with staff and Board, I was a stay-at-home mom, absorbing the perspective of our children's wonderful preschool—as a parent helper, a board member, and briefly as a teacher. Its name—Charlestown Play House—captures the founder's vision of "love and respect for children" and learning through play. As you all were laying the foundations for DAP, I was tiptoeing into graduate study in child development and early education. The department's strong developmental emphasis reinforced my early leanings, with a dissertation on young children's emotional strengths, needs, and coping strategies during everyday experiences.

Degree in hand, starting in the early 1980s, I entered academia, teaching child development while drawing upon the resources of a play-oriented lab school, supervising student teachers, and—hugely unprepared—teaching early childhood curriculum. Within the department, we pondered whether it would help or harm our lab school's children to bring computers into the classroom. (Sue, the dichotomous thinking will sound familiar.) Out in the public school kindergartens, I saw our students' beliefs and practices called into question by their more academically oriented supervising teachers. What great timing: The 1986 DAP position statement and related publications were not only treasured resources but, honestly, were viewed as great ammunition.

SUE: One of the most positive impacts of DAP has been that it served as a unifying framework for defining high-quality programs for children, as it did for you, Marilou. The document has been used to educate teachers and administrators and to update current practitioners. Considering this goal and reality, the major purpose of the 1997 DAP was to correct the problems created by the 1987 position. Among the most impactful changes were:

1. Defining DAP as an intentional decision-making process by teachers based on three core considerations: knowledge of child development and learning in general; what is learned about each individual child; and knowledge of the social and cultural context in which children live. Emphasizing intentional teaching was essential to address the oversimplification of the teacher's role created by the two columns, which were deleted from the official "position statement" but included as examples. In 2009, the "Inappropriate" column was renamed "In contrast." In the 2022 book, the columns remain but are now titled "Examples of developmentally appropriate practices" and "Examples of practices to avoid."
2. Significantly greater emphasis on the role of culture in development and learning, which had been the biggest omission and flaw in the previous edition (now fully incorporated in the 2022 DAP).
3. Articulating five guidelines to describe the complex role of the teacher.
4. Calling for the field to move from *either/or* to *both/and* thinking.

As I said before, the columns not only oversimplified the complex role of the teacher but perpetuated false dichotomies that continue to plague the field such as teacher-directed versus child-initiated, play versus academics, active learning versus direct instruction, social-emotional versus cognitive, and so on. I think our emphasis on *both/and* thinking has had a positive impact, but not as much as we intended and have stressed ever since.

MARILOU: Sue, that 1997 position statement was a launching pad for a lot of my work during my 5 years on NAEYC's staff—hardly replacing you, but to a great extent helping implement and further extend that work. As examples from that period, I think of NAEYC's collaboration with the National Council of Teachers of Mathematics (NCTM) on a joint position statement; similar collaboration with the National Association of Early Childhood Specialists in State Departments of Education (NAECS/SDE) on a position statement on early learning standards (endorsed by, among others, the National Association of Elementary School Principals); and a major revision and extension of NAEYC's position on curriculum, assessment, and program evaluation, with close involvement from the early childhood special education community. Looking back, I can see consistent attention to *both/and* thinking: Teachers can aim *both* to support children's social competence *and* their foundational understanding of mathematics. State early learning standards can *both* contribute to children's educational success *and* use those standards to emphasize significant, developmentally appropriate content. As I'll note later, these kinds of connections, and the resources you describe below, may have extended the visibility, leadership, and reach of NAEYC's DAP work.

SUE: Because the 1997 version was so significantly different from the previous one, we developed a live satellite television course called *The Leading Edge* to educate affiliate leaders, teacher educators, and trainers about the major changes. We used mental models, videos, and a diverse panel of experts to communicate clearly. *The Leading Edge* was very well received, and after 25 years, I still hear positive comments about it.

Given those fundamental changes in the 1997 edition, the 2009 version essentially built on and updated it. In addition to current research, the critical issues it addressed were:

1. Reducing learning gaps and increasing the achievement of all children;
2. Creating improved, better education for preschool and elementary children (improving curriculum and alignment); and
3. Recognizing teacher knowledge and decision-making as vital to educational effectiveness.

DAP had always been about *how* to teach, not *what* to teach. The 2009 DAP addressed this imbalance by incorporating the content of the curriculum, as did your work with NCTM on early mathematics and guidelines for curriculum, Marilou. However, the 2009 focus on the achievement gap was subsequently criticized for promoting a deficit model of children, particularly for children from historically marginalized groups and children experiencing poverty. This deficit model was replaced by a strengths-based emphasis in the 2022 DAP.

The positive impact and strengths of the 2022 DAP were immediately apparent. The document builds on the basic framework of the 1997 version, but every aspect of it demands that early childhood education promote and be responsive to diversity, equity, and inclusion. A commission of 33 diverse experts simultaneously contributed to the development of both the 2019 position statement on *Advancing Equity in Early Childhood Education* and the revised DAP. In addition, the 2022 book is the work of more than 35 diverse authors. It seems likely that the positive impact of the document will continue for the anticipated decade. However, given the rapidly expanding knowledge base and increasingly diverse cultural contexts in which children, families, and educators live and programs operate, such a prediction is far from a certainty.

WHAT HAVE BEEN THE CHALLENGES TO THE STATEMENT OVER THE ENSUING YEARS? HOW HAVE CHALLENGES IMPACTED THE STATEMENT AND ITS INFLUENCE?

SUE: A fundamental lesson I learned from Carol Day when we worked on the 1997 revision was in her words, "The solution to every problem contains the seeds of a new problem." Each revision was intended to address the prevailing issues at the time and correct the problems of the previous edition, but subsequently created others. Many times over the years I have said that if at the beginning we knew the influence DAP was going to have, we would have been much more careful.

Each iteration of DAP was significantly impacted by the numerous challenges and hotly debated critiques it received. Critiques of DAP regularly appeared in books and articles, as well as in point-counterpoint sessions at conferences. The major challenges to the 1987 version were:

1. Lack of awareness and responsiveness to the significant role of culture in development and learning, perpetuating white middle-class bias.
2. Overemphasis on child development and underemphasis on curriculum. This was the first major critique, published in *Early Education and Development* in 1991 [volume 2, issue 2].
3. Passivity of the teacher's role, with too much emphasis on child-initiated learning and play.

4. Omission of Vygotsky's social construction of knowledge among children and teachers.
5. Overemphasis on the individual child, with bias toward an individualistic rather than an interdependent cultural orientation.
6. Failure to include proven effective practices for children with disabilities.
7. Outdated, naïve perspective on the role of families.

MARILOU: Without question, I agree (as someone who was then only marginally connected with NAEYC) about the challenges you've identified here. How about I take a few paragraphs to broaden the frame a bit?

At the same time as, and well before, the development of the revised 1997 DAP, research on child development and early education was becoming more inclusive of many of the perspectives you've identified above (and I know that *you*, as a developmentalist, know this!). Yes, many professional groups had strong objections to the 1987 DAP. Some of these critiques were products of core beliefs or ideologies; others were informed by emerging research on aspects of early development that previously had been understudied or underrepresented in the literature.

I do think that professional organizations—the one you and I have been most closely identified with, as well as others—are apt to have a sort of guild mentality or, another metaphor, tend to circle their organizational wagons around dearly held tenets. I have admired the way that NAEYC, well before my closer involvement, became open to not only addressing outside challenges but also has been proactive in creating opportunities for fresh collective thinking.

SUE: Very true, Marilou. Historically, NAEYC has welcomed and been responsive to wide-ranging, disparate perspectives, although it may not seem so to some audiences, since much of NAEYC's work has been standard-setting. Frankly, we were naïve because we didn't expect that DAP would draw the international attention it received (including numerous translations). In hindsight, we should have been wiser, given that the 1987 DAP position statement implied universals of development and uniform practices for all children.

From that international perspective, much of the criticism came from early adherents of the Reggio Emilia approach. Other critical groups were early childhood special educators (Division of Early Childhood), the National Black Child Development Institute, and the EC interest group of the National Association for Bilingual Education. Most critical of all were scholars who are members of Reconceptualizing Early Childhood Education (RECE). Their mission was and is to challenge mainstream assumptions about how children learn and grow, particularly universal prescriptions for best practice that ignore the diverse contexts and conditions in which children live, of which DAP was the most obvious example.

In 1994, a particularly influential book—*Diversity and Developmentally Appropriate Practices: Challenges for Early Childhood Education* (Teachers College Press), edited by Bruce Mallory and Rebecca New—included chapters by several Reconceptualists. Around that time, there was a well-attended session at NAEYC where Lilian Katz and I debated Rebecca and Bruce. Becky first introduced Reggio Emilia to the United States and critiqued DAP for its weaknesses regarding culture and in comparison to the high quality of practice observed in Reggio programs. Bruce critiqued the document from the special education perspective. At the end of the debate, attendees came up to me and Lilian and said, "You won!" This was extremely disturbing to me because Becky and Bruce were right. The position statement was inadequate for all the reasons they described. I knew that we had to address the critiques because DAP was so widely distributed and embraced. I stopped being defensive and started listening to all their points of view. I went to conferences and met individually with diverse groups and held listening sessions (during which many people yelled at me as NAEYC's representative).

After visiting Reggio in 1993, I was even more determined to significantly revise DAP. We formed a diverse committee to lead the work, purposely including some of its severest critics: Barbara Bowman, Carol Brunson Day, Victoria Fu, Lilian Katz, Becky New, Teresa Rosegrant (my friend and Ph.D.-qualified kindergarten teacher), and Deborah Ziegler (representing DEC). We worked together for 3 years to conceptualize and write the 1997 DAP.

Not long after the 1997 version was published, the International Reading Association was critical because it didn't say enough about early literacy. As mentioned previously, DAP had always been relatively silent on curriculum content. But regarding literacy, this was a very valid concern because for years preschool teachers had declared that teaching the alphabet is developmentally inappropriate. NAEYC and IRA (now the International Literacy Association) agreed on a joint position statement, *Learning to Read and Write: Developmentally Appropriate Practice* [naeyc.org]. (Jack Pikulski, then IRA president, couldn't believe that NAEYC held open hearings where people came to the mike and yelled at us.)

Marilou, you won't be surprised to hear that I tend to view life through the lens of a developmentalist. Human development, as well as the development of professional organizations, is marked by both continuity and change. The same is true of the evolution of DAP. At times, it contributed to significant change, and at other times it reflected continuity with the past. In fact, each edition of DAP has represented both continuity and change simultaneously. For example, the 2022 DAP demonstrates continuity by building on the conceptual framework of the 1997 document. It frames DAP as an intentional decision-making process based on three core considerations (now called commonality, individuality, and context), and continues to describe the role of the teacher with five guidelines: creating a caring, equitable community of learners; reciprocal partnerships with families; teaching; curriculum; and observation and assessment. At the same time, the current document is significantly different because it is closely aligned with the [2019 NAEYC] statement on *Advancing Equity in Early Childhood Education*. Cultural context frames the entire document, including all the principles of learning and development that guide practice, and includes the importance of considering the cultural contexts of educators and the program itself.

MARILOU: Loud cheers coming from here! The central place of cultural contexts and equity within 2022 DAP certainly continues NAEYC's longstanding commitments, but it also responds to the growing interdisciplinary body of research, and the growing visibility of that research, on the sources and lasting effects of minoritization, bias, and inequities in the lives of children and families. At the same time, research is confirming our conviction that children and their families—from every culture and community—embody diverse, often unique strengths. That theme, too, is strongly represented in the 2022 DAP.

As you know, since leaving NAEYC, I've spent much time in what the World Bank calls low- and middle-income countries—Indonesia, Bangladesh, Papua New Guinea, and Rwanda, to name a few. My experiences there are affirmed by the themes of the 2022 DAP. Those experiences have also brought me face-to-face with the realities of contextual issues in "translating" DAP principles and practices. Childrearing norms, religious traditions, culturally driven health practices, educational beliefs—all of these and others tend to call into question what seemed to "work" in U.S. settings, including professional development contexts. Honestly, the 1987 dichotomous statements of appropriate and inappropriate practices are more understandable and appealing to village teachers, and their trainers, coming from authoritarian traditions than the more nuanced, complex (and to us, more accurate) DAP framings that have followed.

SUE: In many ways, defining DAP is an impossible task. Over the years the books got longer and longer, going from 60 pages in 1986 to 342 in 2022. In fact, my very favorite part of the 2022 version is this succinct statement: "NAEYC defines developmentally appropriate practice as methods that promote each child's optimal development and learning through a strengths-based, play-based approach to joyful engaged learning" [see 2020 position statement online].

At the same time, despite (and perhaps because of) the call to embrace diverse cultural contexts, DAP continues to present inherent contradictions. For example, the document calls for true responsiveness to families' cultural preferences for their children's care and education. And yet, what if families do not want a play-based approach but rather a strong emphasis on didactic instruction in academic skills to prepare their children for success in school? Many other paradoxes exist, such as those Marilou cited. Although the position statement explicitly rejects the concept of best practice, its very existence requires resolving the contradictions that it creates.

HOW HAS DAP INFLUENCED CLASSROOM PRACTICES AND TEACHER PREPARATION?

MARILOU: There's an impossible question, at least for me! Most of us would think it likely that there have been such influences, but how would one know, and how would one disentangle the specific influence of DAP from other multiple, interrelated, and perhaps indistinguishable influences? So let me try to answer the question from that perspective.

Influences on Classroom Practices: As Sue said, back in 1986, DAP grew out of NAEYC's efforts to clarify what the phrase "developmentally appropriate practices" meant in the context of quality features essential to early childhood program accreditation. Early in my academic career, I became involved in a 2-year grant-funded study called the Academic Environments Project. With colleagues Leslie Rescorla and Kathy Hirsh-Pasek, I examined parents' and teachers' attitudes about the role of academic instruction at home and in preschool. We planned to focus on a group of middle-class families that chose to enroll their children in preschools regarded by reputation as either "play-oriented" or "academic." But we found *no* observational measures that were relevant to our research aims.

Sue, that's when I turned to you. I remember sitting in my kitchen, tentatively involved in my first major grant, calling NAEYC headquarters with great trepidation. Surely *someone* must have operationalized what were then called the "DAP Guidelines"? Sue answered with another *no*, but added a career-changing piece of advice: "So why don't you do it yourselves?" And we did.

The Classroom Practices Inventory (CPI) included specific, observable items adapted from and closely aligned with those DAP Guidelines. We used the CPI to verify core differences between the classrooms and to correlate observed practices with factors including teachers' and parents' belief systems. Interest in the measure has continued; to my surprise, when Googling for this chapter, I found new uses floating up as recently as 2021.

However, this kind of research tells us little about the "influences" of DAP on what teachers do in their classrooms. The influence of a single document or position statement, whether it be the Green Book of the 1980s or later NAEYC revisions and publications, remains impossible to determine. Today, the question has become even more difficult to answer. Undoubtedly, many educators continue to rely on DAP materials as guides to practice, but resources for classroom teachers, administrators, and professional development providers have multiplied exponentially. Some of these explicitly include or draw on DAP core concepts and themes; others do not. How could one say with certainty, "Aha! *That's* what DAP has done and is doing to improve quality practices"?

SUE: I agree completely, Marilou. It is impossible to accurately "measure" the impact of DAP. Since the first edition, the book has been the all-time bestseller among NAEYC's publications. And I would venture to guess that it is among the most frequently cited references in early childhood articles and books. None of that measures its true impact. The basic research question regarding any educational practice is: Does it work? Is this practice effective in helping children achieve important learning and developmental outcomes and succeed in school and life? Does the practice support the development and learning of diverse, individual children?

One of my concerns over the years has been the impossibility of demonstrating DAP's effectiveness because so many practices are incorporated in the statement. Nevertheless, there is a large body of research on individual practices that are core elements of DAP, such as the importance of positive teacher-child relationships; the diverse benefits of various types of play; intentional teaching of literacy and mathematics skills and knowledge; effective ways to promote social skills and peer interactions, self-regulation, and executive function; and much more. DAP simply includes too many practices and principles to demonstrate that it "works"—an overarching weakness that leaves it justifiably subject to criticism.

MARILOU: It occurs to me that a problem has been that DAP has been considered as an "it," rather than—as you indicate—a set of interrelated but distinct practices that can be examined for effectiveness separately but also (at least not easily) together. In its statements, DEC (the Division for Early Childhood of the Council for Exceptional Children) has taken the approach of using the plural: "Recommended Practices" in early intervention and early childhood special education. It's worth considering whether this decision traded off a greater degree of coherence for a more specific and grounded evidence base.

Turning to the second, interrelated part of this question—DAP's influences on teacher preparation—well, before I joined the NAEYC staff, I was immersed in early childhood teacher education. I taught undergraduates and supervised practicum students. Later, I was a member of NAEYC's Professional Development Panel, reviewing higher education programs for approval. Although they were not initially based on DAP—in fact, preceding that position, over time NAEYC's Teacher Education Guidelines were intentionally aligned with DAP. Today they continue to reflect that alignment. The teacher education guidelines, now called Professional Standards and Competencies, were crucially important to me as a teacher educator. And first as a reviewer of NAEYC teacher education programs through the Professional Development Panel, and then for 6 years on the NAEYC staff, I was able to see the extent to which the NAEYC standards were reflected in what was reported by those higher education institutions applying for accreditation. Most programs seemed to reflect the emphases of the NAEYC standards. But many did not, at least judging from the limited documentation that programs were required to submit at that time, primarily course syllabi. Especially concerning was the tendency of many programs to overlook the importance of key areas (all related to DAP and the NAEYC professional preparation standards), notably a focus on appropriate assessment of children's progress and on partnerships with families.

Today, we have a better—or at least more complex—sense of the multiple contexts and constraints within which higher education programs operate. State licensure and degree requirements, "academic homes" housing early childhood programs, institutional funding, and a host of other factors can potentially enhance, or too often further diminish, the extent to which the preparation of early childhood professionals is affected by specific DAP features.

As I look at my past writings about early childhood teacher preparation, I read a lot of doom and gloom. In 2012, my colleagues and I raised at least two major concerns: (a) a lack of rigorous, fine-grained research that can identify which *specific features* of higher education (here one can include DAP) contribute to the use of practices leading to positive outcomes for children—and how to implement those features; and (b) a lack of relevant support for early childhood faculty, building their capacity to use sound content and effective pedagogy as they, in turn, support future educators. A decade later, these concerns persist and may have deepened. The potential for DAP's impact remains, I believe, but it is yet to be clearly seen.

SUE: I share your concerns about teacher education and have for a long time. My first assignment when I joined the NAEYC staff in 1981 was to develop their Teacher Education Guidelines for baccalaureate programs and subsequently for associate, master's, and Ph.D. programs. I also administered the National Council for Accreditation of Teacher Education (NCATE) reviews, which is where our paths crossed most closely during those years. Of course, we constantly encountered widespread variance in program quality and content coverage that resulted in part from widely varying definitions of "early childhood" in state licensure/certification standards. We wrote a joint position on EC teacher certification with the Association of Teacher Educators (ATE) advocating for birth through age 8 licensure. Unfortunately, the situation has only gotten worse since then. As for DAP's role in teacher education, faculty have often assigned it as a textbook or at least a supplemental resource, which accounts in some way for its high volume of sales. As for how it is used and interpreted in teacher preparation programs, to my knowledge there is no clear evidence to answer that question.

In fact, the continuing need to improve and enhance the consistency of teacher education is what led NAEYC to launch the Professional Development Institute in 1991, now called Professional Learning Institute or PLI. Throughout the 1980s, NAEYC had focused on improving the quality of programs for young children by developing accreditation and promulgating DAP. Obviously that goal could not be achieved without well-qualified teachers. In addition, it was clear that the interests and needs of the teacher education community were not well served at the annual conference. They attended as presenters but did not find enough sessions that focused on their own professional development and learning. Hence, the first PLI was held in Los Angeles in 1991. Without precedent to guide us, we planned for 300 conferees, and more than 600 attended. Barbara Willer and I wrote concept papers to provide a vision for the work, one of which proposed a career lattice for the field that has since entered the lexicon seamlessly. Without relating the PLI history in detail, I think it's safe to say that much of that work more than 2 decades ago prefigured Transforming the Workforce and the Power to the Profession initiative that NAEYC now leads.

MARILOU: I so agree about the terrific yearly event then called the Professional Development Institute. Before I joined the NAEYC staff, the Institute was my professional "home" for continuous learning and lasting connections. The meeting has evolved in recent years, I'm sure for pragmatic/economic reasons, into something more generic and more similar to the Annual Conference. Yet within and connected to the Professional Learning Institute remain important elements that you, Sue, set into motion. So, thank you!

WHAT HAS BEEN THE MOST IMPORTANT AND LASTING IMPACT OF DAP? AND WHAT DO WE NEED IN THE FUTURE?

MARILOU: Sue, what on earth did you and your colleagues set in motion in 1986, and what has been its effect? You've referred to this issue earlier, and my sense is that we agree that it seems impossible to measure DAP's impact in any simple, straightforward way. But maybe this difficulty actually shows its complex, largely unmeasured impact over almost 40 years.

To put it metaphorically, one might think of the impact of DAP as an enormous stone—the DAP boulder?—dropped into the center of a large body of water; I imagine a lake with many inlets and streams running into it. How could you identify the most important impact of that boulder? Is it the big splash at the very beginning, or is it what happens over time? The effects may be very noticeable at first, with the boulder generating major waves and maybe even changing some of the shoreline. Over time (I'm imagining time-lapse photography here), the circle of waves becomes wider, but the ripples become smaller and harder to distinguish from other wavelets and currents.

Leaving the metaphor, to me that change doesn't mean that DAP's impact has disappeared, but rather that its influence has become indistinguishable from a complex network of other influences that, in turn, have undoubtedly been impacted by that pretty massive stone.

But if I had to boil down DAP's impact to one sentence, let me try this on for size: *DAP has been a powerful stimulus for dynamic dialogues leading to continuous growth and (often?) innovation.* As you have said here and elsewhere, Sue, these dialogues (call them challenges if you will) emerged from the beginning, as the initial position statement pushed back against the use of narrowly academic content and didactic methods in the preschool years. The dialogues have continued not just within NAEYC and not just within the early childhood field. They have been seen and continue to be seen in policymakers' clashes over the meaning and measurement of school readiness, the content of early learning standards, the uses of assessment with diverse learners and in diverse contexts, the effects on children of bias and injustice, and many more. Within these kinds of policy-and-practice dialogues, DAP's core concepts and principles continue to stimulate and inform the debates, although the "developmentally appropriate practice" terminology may never be referenced.

SUE: Marilou, I love metaphors, and I think yours of DAP as a large stone that generated countless waves both large and small is inspired. And I couldn't agree more that perhaps the greatest contribution of DAP has been to generate dialogues and heated arguments (several of which I previously described) that led to major reconceptualizations and revisions in the statement. Without overstating its impact, I think its lasting effect has been to lift up and widely disseminate essential aspects of the knowledge base that have the potential to enhance professional learning of educators and improve learning experiences and outcomes for vast numbers of young children. Of course, the early childhood field has been transformed since DAP was first published almost 40 years ago. However, DAP has contributed to that transformation at least in part because of its extremely wide distribution, relatively concise compilation of the current knowledge base, and the imprimatur of the largest early childhood professional organization in the world.

MARILOU: Before turning to the second part of this question (What do we need for the future?), one quick comment on what you just said: I have worried about the term "the knowledge base." You,

I, and many others know that the term can be misleading if people conclude that there is an immutable body of knowledge underpinning what is called "DAP." Instead, the relevant knowledge base for early childhood has undergone expansion because of new research, new professional insights, and new early childhood contexts and issues—and in turn that expansion has contributed to the new conceptualizations embodied in later revisions of DAP.

Now to that question about what we need for the future. Let me propose two ideas—and no doubt you'll propose others, Sue: (1) I suggest that what may be needed is the *disappearance* of the term "DAP." Bear with me here: If DAP's most powerful concepts and principles, in all their complexity, become deeply integrated into early childhood policy and practice, the terminology may become not only unnecessary but also an obstacle to consensus and effective implementation. (2) New leadership structures and pipelines are essential if the first part of my wish list is to become a reality—the infusion of "DAP" into the widest possible corners of the early childhood world. I can't help emphasizing that Sue—for all her generous credit to others within and beyond NAEYC—has often been that leader. And yes, a core group of other early childhood thought leaders and policymakers—primarily identified with NAEYC—have served to disseminate, advocate, study, and generally add value. But that is not a sustainable system. As greater diffusion of the core concepts and principles associated with DAP occurs, they must be articulated and advocated by new, emerging leaders who may not necessarily have been among DAP's "mainstream." New generations of leaders from diverse, often marginalized groups, from often-overlooked disciplines, and from a wide range of professional identities may create a new language in which to talk about DAP and new contexts in which DAP's impact can continue and expand.

SUE: Marilou, fortunately the new generation of leaders that you describe are already engaged in this much-needed work, among whom are the 35 diverse scholars who developed the two recent position statements and wrote the 2022 DAP book. In addition, you've identified an issue that has arisen each time DAP has been revised: Should the term be changed? We discussed this during the second and third editions, and although I was not involved in the most recent revision, I know the issue was seriously debated. The fundamental problem with "developmentally appropriate practice" is that the word "appropriate" is always culturally defined and determined. From its earliest inception, DAP was justifiably criticized for narrowly representing white middle-class values and lacking responsiveness to cultural and linguistic diversity. The notion that one set of teaching practices is "appropriate" for all children has been problematic from the start. We seriously debated changing the term in the 1997 edition but rejected the notion because the most important reason for revising the document was to correct the errors and misinterpretations of the 1987 edition. By 2009, the terminology had become so deeply rooted in the early childhood lexicon that changing it became an almost insurmountable obstacle. The most recent edition continues to use DAP because the larger purpose is not only to reflect current knowledge but, most importantly, to redefine and fully align the concept and book with the 2019 *Advancing Equity in Early Childhood Programs* position statement.

However, the current DAP position clearly states that it rejects the notion of "best practice" because no one set of practices can be deemed "best" for each and every child regardless of culture, race, ethnicity, language, gender, disability/ability, or social background. Despite this caution, it is unlikely that NAEYC will drop or change the term DAP in the near future. Peruse their website, read the journal, or attend their conferences, and you will see that DAP has essentially become the Association's brand.

But as you point out, Marilou, "practices" may be a better, more accurate term as it was used by DEC and in the title of Mallory and New's critical book (*Diversity and Developmentally Appropriate Practices*). Personally, I've often thought of developmentally appropriate *practice* as a verb, not a noun, similar to how doctors *practice* medicine—drawing on a vast and changing knowledge base requiring professional decisions about individual people within their context at a particular time.

In fact, I have begun to adopt diverse language to articulate the concept. Among the terms I find useful are *developmentally aligned*, *developmentally informed*, and *developmentally attuned*. I also now prefer the term *effective practice* because as far back as the 1997 edition, we stated that practices cannot be developmentally appropriate unless they *contribute* to children's development and learning, and that includes their ability to function well and succeed in their own linguistic and cultural contexts. Presently, we need to emphasize that practices cannot be developmentally appropriate unless they are *equitable*—meaning that children do not receive the "same" or equal experiences but rather what they specifically need to build on their strengths and support their optimal development and learning. One final word about terminology. The dictionary defines *appropriate* as "suitable or right for a particular situation or purpose," which I interpret as *not* suitable or right for *every* purpose or situation.

I want to conclude by saying that although my name has been linked to DAP since its inception, my work was part of my job as Director of Professional Development at NAEYC. DAP has always represented the expertise, wisdom, experience, and input of literally hundreds of people. To be honest, I have received far too much credit (and frankly blame) over the years. I'm pleased to have an opportunity to have this conversation with you, Marilou, since your work has both intersected with and diverged from my own. I just wish we could have included my dear friends and colleagues, Marilyn M. Smith and Carol Copple, who sadly are no longer with us. Their work and leadership were essential to the development and evolution of DAP and to my professional life.

MARILOU: I want to leave you with the last word except for an amen from a place of admiration and friendship.

Reflections on the Developmentally Appropriate Practice Position Statement of the National Association for the Education of Young Children Conversation

Nancy E. Barbour

Sue and Marilou have taken us on a journey through almost 4 decades as they discuss the Developmentally Appropriate Practice (DAP) document produced by the National Association for the Education of Young Children (NAEYC). This historical journey did not happen in the absence of important historical contexts. Perhaps it is critical to add this layer for an even deeper understanding of the DAP story.

When Head Start began in 1965, there was a clear mission: "The federal government would enable local communities to provide poor and minority children with the early experiences that would equip them to start school on par with their middle-class peers" (Zigler & Styfco, 2004). This was a bold effort toward equality. However, there were critical questions: Did we have a clear theoretical base for a solid, appropriate early childhood curriculum to level the playing field? Scholars like Miller and Dyer (1975) attempted to address the question of "best approach" by systematically assessing different theoretically based curricula for educational impact. Their results lacked definitive support for one successful approach. Subsequent attempts have had similar results.

A little more than a decade later, NAEYC took on the task of guiding the field from a slightly different perspective, focusing on "best practice" rather than specific curricula. Sue describes the early, collaborative process of creating the DAP document as a response to the pushdown curriculum by offering teachers practical guidance. It was also an attempt to elevate the status of the marginalized field of early education. By defining what was developmentally appropriate and what was not developmentally appropriate, NAEYC provided the 1987 position statement as a road map for teachers and teacher educators. But what they really did, according to Sue and Marilou, was to begin decades-long conversations (or maybe debates?) that have created growth, nuanced thinking, and research paths. These debates and challenges have not always been cordial or kind, but they seem to have been the impetus for each of the subsequent iterations of DAP. The most recent challenge to DAP has come from a more political and, perhaps, less informed perspective. More on that later.

Marilou describes how practical the DAP statement was for her as a teacher of young children. Yet this first iteration, though helpful to many, was lacking for others. The DAP versus DIP (developmentally inappropriate) dichotomy identified in the document made many uncomfortable. A primary question from the field was: Who decides what knowledge, values, and goals are of most importance in determining what developmentally appropriate practice is?

In 1994, Mallory and New pulled together many of the critics, as well as supporters, of DAP to address the concerns that were being debated around the country. The historical context seemed to set the stage. Piagetian theory was being questioned and Vygotskian theory revisited. Children with special needs became a priority with both PL 94–142 in 1975 and IDEA in 1990. The contributing authors identified their concerns: the absence of culture and its impact on development, the overreliance on child development as defining curriculum, the overemphasis of Piagetian theory with the omission of Vygotsky, the seeming passivity of the teachers' defined role, the overemphasis on individuality rather than interdependence, the absence of inclusiveness, and the narrow view of families' roles in early education. Many of those challenging the first version of DAP formed the Reconceptualist movement in early childhood. The ideas emerging from this group provided counterpoints to the NAEYC work.

Subsequent revisions to DAP in 1997, 2009, and 2022 have tried to address the critiques coming from the field. Sue reminds us that each of these versions were NAEYC position statements with a vetting process involving broad input. Nonetheless, with each revision came new challenges. As Sue quotes Carol Day: "The solution to every problem contains the seeds of a new problem." And with each decade, historical context colored the revisions.

The first revision, in a time of challenges to business as usual, made attempts to address the role of the teacher by envisioning the teacher as decision-maker. The revisions also attempted to address culture and atypical development by emphasizing individual differences in development and factors influencing these differences. The revision did not address the discomfort with the DAP/DIP dichotomy. According to Sue, this controversial piece may have been what gave the document its standing and focus in the field. Nonetheless, there continued to be lively discussion from those who believed DAP had not gone far enough in changing.

The third revision, taking shape through the early 2000s, focused on curricular content, perhaps as a reflection of the federal efforts coming out of Education Goals 2000. Marilou describes NAEYC's collaborations with national organizations such as NCTM and IRA (now ILA) that were then reflected in the 2009 document. Yet discussion of learning gaps underpinning Goals 2000 was seen as promoting deficit models of childhood.

The most recent revision of the DAP position statement responded to a national climate of diversity, equity, and inclusion as important goals broadly and for early childhood specifically. The DAP document takes a strong position on a strengths-based view of young children as well as the importance of culture, diversity, and individual differences/needs. Once again, the document has unleashed critique, this time from an unexpected political perspective.

In April 2023, the Alabama governor removed the DAP book from prekindergarten classrooms because it addressed the issue of systemic racism and inclusion of LGBTQIA+ families in its guidance for early childhood teachers. The governor fired the Secretary of the Department of Early Childhood Education for providing Alabama teachers with this "woke" document and ordered it removed from teachers' classrooms. Though the DAP document has never been intended as a curriculum, it seems to have been perceived as that by the Alabama governor. Though we may agree that education is a political act, have we considered the political impact of DAP over time? This is the first political critique of the DAP document. It remains to be seen whether this response will be echoed in other state legislatures or higher education institutions. Sue and Marilou's dialogue preceded this event, so they did not have an opportunity to air their concerns.

As I consider this long history of DAP, I am amazed by the energy, movement, and force it has had on me as a teacher educator and scholar in the field. Like Marilou and others, the "Green Book" was an essential tool in my teacher education life and in my academic writing life. Likewise, the influence of DAP is echoed in almost every one of the conversations in this volume. Over the years, DAP became a brand for NAEYC both here and abroad. But has DAP identified explicit values and goals? Is this why those in the field have widely differing opinions?

So, what will be or should be the future of DAP? Sue and Marilou agree that we need to do more "fine-grained research" to understand what aspects of professional preparation are important and make positive impacts. The original goal of elevating what has been a marginalized field has not been realized, but there are small steps like the effort of Power to the Profession. Likewise, the original goal of heading off the pushdown of curriculum, according to Sue, has not been successful over the decades.

Marilou suggests that perhaps we should stop using the label DAP. However, Sue suggests instead that we think of it as a verb rather than a noun. In any case, I believe that DAP will have a long shelf life, perhaps long after we are gone. However, it is intriguing to think about what the next iterations of DAP will bring. Will it survive the politically motivated attack from outside the field? I prefer to think of Marilou's image of the boulder falling into the water and rippling out through various rivers and streams, continuing over time to change the landscape of early childhood practice.

QUESTIONS FOR DISCUSSION

1. Have the DAP position statements been a boon or a hindrance to advancing the status of the early childhood profession? In what ways?
2. What are the implicit and explicit values and goals underlying DAP?
3. How might you use the most current DAP document in your work with young children?

FOR FURTHER READING

Bredekamp, S. (2016). *Effective practices in early childhood education: Building a foundation*. Pearson.

Brown, C. P. (2021). *Resisting the kinder-race: Restoring the joy to early learning*. Teachers College Press.

Hyson, M. C., Hirsh-Pasek, K., & Rescorla, L. (1990). The classroom practices inventory: An observation instrument based on NAEYC's guidelines for developmentally appropriate practices for 4- and 5-year-old children. *Early Childhood Research Quarterly, 5*, 475–494.

Mallory, B. L., & New, R. S. (1994). *Diversity and developmentally appropriate practices: Challenges for early childhood education.* Teachers College Press.

Miller, L. B., & Dyer, J. L. (1975). Four preschool programs: Their dimensions and effects. *Monographs of the Society for Research in Child Development*, 162 (40), 5–6.

NAEYC. (1987, 1997, 2009, 2022). *Developmentally appropriate practice.* Author.

Zigler, E., & Styfco, S. J. (2004). *The Head Start debates*. Brookes.

CHAPTER 4

The Place of Play in Early Childhood Education

Jaipaul L. Roopnarine and Jeffrey Trawick-Smith

Jaipaul L. Roopnarine is the Pearl S. Falk Professor of Human Development at Syracuse University, Syracuse, New York, and Professor Extraordinary of Developmental Psychology at Anton de Kom University of Suriname, Paramaribo. He was a Fulbright scholar at the University of the West Indies, Trinidad and Tobago, and has held visiting appointments at different universities across the world. His research interests include father–child relationships across cultures, mental health in Caribbean families and children, early childhood education in international perspective, children's play across cultures, and immigrant families and schooling. He has published several volumes on culture and development (e.g., *Caribbean Psychology: Indigenous Contributions to a Global Discipline*; *Fathering in Cultural Contexts: Developmental and Clinical Issues)* and has published extensively in developmental psychology and childhood development journals. He is the current editor-in-chief of the *Caribbean Journal of Psychology.*

Jeffrey Trawick-Smith was the inaugural Phyllis Waite Endowed Chair and currently serves as a research consultant in the Center for Early Childhood Education at Eastern Connecticut State University. He has authored or edited seven books and 70 articles in refereed journals, most related to young children's play, development, and culture. Two of his books, *Young Children's Play: Development, Disabilities, and Diversity* and *Early Childhood Development: A Multicultural Perspective,* are read around the world and have been translated into several languages. He has conducted 42 empirical studies of young children, including those funded by the U.S. Department of Education, the U.S. Department of Defense, and the

Spencer Foundation. He has received recognition and awards for his scholarship from the American Educational Research Association and the National Association of Early Childhood Teacher Educators. He is a former preschool and kindergarten teacher and director of a child development center.

WHAT SHIFTS HAVE YOU SEEN OVER YOUR CAREER IN THE PLACE OF PLAY IN EARLY CHILDHOOD EDUCATION?

JAIPAUL: As a child growing up in British Guiana (Guyana), I played in nearby streams, in treetops, and by the seaside. I remember the joy I encountered from jumping into the waves at the local beach, swinging from the branches of trees, and building mud slides at the edges of canals that emptied into the nearby Corentyne River. Whether in the heat of the tropical sun or during torrential downpours, these playful activities became a central part of my childhood. At times, I pursued these activities alone. On most occasions, though, they involved other children whose daily lives mirrored the challenges I faced: food insecurity, lack of educational and play materials, poor access to health care, and meager economic resources. Not unlike children living in poverty-stricken circumstances in other cultural communities across the world, some playful activities were embedded in work. Regardless of the context or weather conditions, play in natural settings permitted me and other children a temporary escape from the abject poverty we experienced daily and from the oppressive conditions that British colonialism imposed on the different ethnic groups in Guyana (e.g., Indigenous, and descendants of enslaved people and indentured laborers).

It is difficult for anyone to imagine that the playful activities of childhood in the context of difficult circumstances would become a central feature of their academic career. I was drawn to the psychological sciences in my early training and in graduate school at the University of Wisconsin-Madison. An undergraduate course in child psychology and a graduate course on play and early childhood education assisted in steering me toward exploring risk and protective factors and developmental pathways to childhood development. At that time, there was limited focus on cultural developmental pathways in determining links between parent-child interactions and childhood development. Nor were cultural beliefs and processes in childhood socialization discussed much in the psychological sciences or early education field.

Although my early efforts to explore the meaning of different modes of play began in a mixed-age laboratory preschool at Wisconsin, it was research on rough-stimulating activities (e.g. rough and tumble play) between fathers and children in different cultural settings that led me to explore parent-child play and the playful activities of young children across cultures. Observations of parent-child play in India, Taiwan, Thailand, and forager groups in Central Africa were instrumental in extending my early conceptions of and the meaning of play for childhood development.

JEFF: Your descriptions of your own play as a child are so rich, Jaipaul. They capture what is most important about play, in my view—that it is what makes childhood joyful. You illustrate in your descriptions how play can be a respite from the challenges faced by children in poverty. All children need to play, but you illustrate how play can be especially important when children and their families are at risk. Your academic contributions, Jaipaul—your observations of the play of children of diverse cultures—have shaped my own view. Reading your research has helped me to realize that not all children play alike and that my original views of play were narrowly restricted to the activities of middle-class American children.

Like you, my interest in play was shaped by my play life as a child. I grew up in a middle-class home in the midwestern United States with many toys, plenty to eat, and lots of kids in our neighborhood to play with. But I was a quiet, withdrawn child with only a couple of true friends. So I was attracted to types of play that allowed me to imagine that I was a more competent, powerful person—pretend and construction play. In both of these play activities, I could lose myself in make-believe roles: a firefighter, a race car driver, a soldier (my father fought in World War II). I carried out play themes with miniature cars, animals, and people. I built imaginary castles with blocks and—in what I found the most exhilarating—knocked them down, pretending to be a giant monster. Note that these play forms have traditionally been valued and frequently observed in the activities of American and European children.

It's easy to understand, then, why, as a preschool and kindergarten teacher, I devoted so much effort to planning and creating dramatic play and block centers in my classrooms. These were the types of play that I loved as a child, so wouldn't they be critical for the development of all children? Later, as a researcher, I continued to be most interested in these types of play. In particular, I began investigating how play materials and teacher-child interactions promote make-believe and more complex building. I was well into my career before I began to broaden my view of play to include the many variations of childhood activity in the world.

JAIPAUL: Although the socioeconomic conditions, access to material and educational resources, and the physical settings of our childhoods were different, play fundamentally served a socioemotional function for both of us. No doubt, the pretend and constructive play activities of your childhood in the midwestern United States permitted opportunities to both escape from and flourish amid emotional challenges. In a similar way, the joy I encountered in the playful activities of childhood in rural Guyana assisted me in emotionally coping with the difficult circumstances associated with daily life. A recurring question in my mind centers around the ameliorative and protective functions of play in reducing risks to young children. That is, what are the cascading effects of play in the context of risk and protective factors for children in different cultural communities? The latter would become a central feature of my recent work on pathways of associations between parent-child play and cognitive and social skills in young children across cultural communities. In essence, I made an early decision to delineate whether the developmental outcomes of different play activities are similar for children in cultural communities across high-, middle-, and low-income countries.

As I became acquainted with the play literature, there was very little on the play of children in other ethnic/cultural groups in the United States or the Global South at the time. This, coupled with the findings of an impressive anthropological study on Aka foragers in the Central African Republic, urged me to consider discourses into culture-specific and pancultural trends in parental beliefs about and the benefits of play for different aspects of childhood development. When I was in graduate school, there was an intriguing debate as to whether rough stimulating play between fathers and children contributed to the development of attachment to fathers. Observations among Aka foragers and other cultural groups around the world (e.g., India, Taiwan, Thailand) would suggest that it may not. This cuts to the heart of my general focus on cultural developmental pathways to childhood development—the concept of equifinality that underlines different processes and potential outcomes to instrumental competence in children and the acquisition of skills necessary for life within the immediate community.

An essential component of my focus on play and childhood development embodies my struggles to connect parent-child play and early education practices. Unlike you, Jeff, I had no direct teaching experiences in early childhood settings. As I worked with government entities and nongovernmental organizations (NGOs) in low- and middle-income countries, I had opportunities to assist in revising national early childhood curricula to essentially make them more developmentally and culturally appropriate. This window ushered in new opportunities to stress the importance of play in early childhood education in Caribbean and other cultural communities. Many early childhood programs in the Caribbean highly value early academic training. Worse yet, parents are of the belief that early academic training is essential for early school success. Much to my regret, these applied aspects of my work came much later in my career.

JEFF: As I read your reflections, Jaipaul, I think about how scholars and teachers did not, for so long, consider the meaning and developmental impact of play for all children around the world or even those of diverse backgrounds within the United States. You offer an interesting example of this: There has been a prevalent belief among researchers and educators that the rough, "stimulating play" that you refer to is developmentally beneficial. You note that this may or may not be the case, depending on a child's cultural and family background. As another example, it was once believed that Korean American preschool children were more "hesitant" and less "sociable" in their play—suggesting that they might have social deficits. Of course, more recent investigations on Korean American children show that they engage in unique, complex, and developmentally beneficial play behaviors that are consistent with the social interactions within their families. One important change in early education over my career, then, is a greater awareness among scholars and many teachers that culture, socioeconomic status, linguistic background, and family life must be considered when interpreting play or supporting it in classrooms.

Your discussion of how play can be a protective factor for children at risk is so important, Jaipaul. As a teacher, I worked with children and families living in the most impoverished neighborhood in Louisville, Kentucky. I observed children in my classroom cope with traumatic experiences through their play. Jaipaul, you have likely come across examples of this in your work in other parts of the world, how important it would be for children living in war zones or towns destroyed by earthquakes to be able to play.

I taught during a different era, when the main purpose of early education was to promote emotional health and social development.

Unfortunately, like you, I am seeing much greater emphasis in schools today in the United States on academic training. A prevalent view in recent years has been that the main purpose of preschool and kindergarten is "school readiness"—that is, achievement of specific academic outcomes. The place of play has been greatly diminished in classrooms in favor of direct instruction. Play in schools now needs to be justified by how it will promote literacy or math.

A good example of this trend is a recent effort to turn play into a literacy experience. Play centers are infused with writing materials and books. As children play, teachers interact with them to enhance their knowledge of print. A more recent concept in the early education literature is *guided play*. In this approach, teachers use play to promote academic skills. In several investigations, children whose teachers asked questions and posed challenges during play learned math concepts. But what children in these studies did not necessarily acquire were emotional well-being or social competence—things that have traditionally been the reasons for play in schools. Given reports of childhood emotional distress during and after the COVID-19 pandemic, I'm particularly worried about displacing play with academics, depriving children of an important protective factor.

JAIPAUL: As we continue to explore different modes of play and their role in early education and childhood development in diverse cultural and ethnic groups, we are beginning to see some similar developmental functions of play across cultural communities. For instance, the socioemotional function of play appears universal. However, as you pointed out, much more emphasis should be placed on how play and developmental pathways to childhood development are connected among families and children in low- and middle-income countries. Children in several cultural communities integrate subsistence and household work with excursions into playful activities that reflect roles they may have to assume later in life. As noted earlier, economic constraints have a significant impact on the ability of parents to meet the cognitive and social needs of children, and the lack of literacy-based materials and objects for play in the home environment can only compound these challenges. We simply have not catalogued children's playful activities and their connections to childhood development in most of the world's cultural communities.

Turning to risk and protective factors, a parallel scenario exists. The function of play in mitigating risks associated with socioeconomic conditions and inadequate play materials and educational resources in home environments, and adverse childhood experiences

(ACEs—mental health issues, abuse and neglect, domestic violence) in the low- and middle-income countries, is far from clear. Can playful activities temper or mediate the effects of these risk factors among children in the low- and middle-income countries? If so, which are the more potent play activities that can reduce psychological risks to young children?

It is my surmise that playful activities can and do lessen the impact of different risk factors on childhood development. My own playful activities during childhood noted at the top of this chapter provided some protective function against risk to my psychological and cognitive development. I applaud the attempts made to examine the play of children in refugee camps, play in war-torn areas, play and poverty, and play and political conflict. The play research and associated theoretical underpinnings can help to extend our understanding of play in the most difficult of circumstances. Note that most of the world's children live in low- and middle-income countries under less than ideal conditions.

In the cultural communities I have studied (e.g., Caribbean, African, and Asian), children play freely in home and community settings. Because early education programs are not readily accessible or available to children in low- and middle-income countries, most of these children's early play experiences occur outside early childhood education settings. Moreover, allocaregivers (e.g., siblings, aunts, uncles, and other, nonkinship members) are active play partners, something not considered in the play literature. Be that as it may, I agree with you and others that play has been and continues to be sidelined for academic work, being tidy, and following rules in the classroom in different cultural communities. The tension between playful learning and rote memorization is palpable. There are efforts to change these practices (e.g., Brazil, Ghana, Trinidad and Tobago).

HOW HAVE THEORETICAL PERSPECTIVES AND SOCIETAL CONTEXTS IMPACTED HOW PLAY IS USED IN CLASSROOMS?

JEFF: The way scholars and educators think about play has changed over the years. As a graduate student, I began to read the work of classic play theorists, whose views were so varied. Some proposed that play is mainly a way that children release pent-up energy. I think about a period as a teacher when my students couldn't go out to play due to bad weather. Once the sun came out, I watched children pour out onto the playground, erupting with joy and laughter. Other theorists, in contrast, suggested that play is a way to acquire greater energy, not to expend it. Day-to-day school life is draining, the thinking went, so children need to "recharge their batteries" through play. I observed this process as a teacher as well, when children seemed to slump and lose interest after a long time of sitting for a story. Play seemed to actually revive them.

There were other, more complex theories long ago. Play is how children learn verbal and nonverbal communication, one theorist proposed. When children are playing, they must communicate to peers, through tone of voice, gestures, and facial expressions, that what they're doing is not real, just pretend. A great example of this is play fighting—an activity of concern to some teachers but enjoyed by children of both genders—in which smiles, silly voices, and laughter show that kicks and punches are not to be taken literally. As we think about classic play theories, we mustn't forget Freud, who described play as a way for children to express feelings, including worries, so as to "bring them to the surface" and manage them. When I think of Freud's view of play, I recall a child in my preschool classroom who would scold and spank the dolls, using harsh, vulgar language. He was trying to gain control over something in his family life that was worrisome. You have suggested, Jaipaul, that play might lessen for this child the deleterious effects of his family's poverty. Like you, I discovered the emotional benefits of play as a child and have always been drawn to theories of play that emphasize its importance to mental health.

These early theorists varied in their views, but most assumed that play was something natural and necessary that all children pursue on their own. For most of my teaching career and in my early research, I shared the perspective that play is simply something children *must* do to enjoy childhood—full stop. To be honest, I still feel this way.

JAIPUAL: As sound as they may have been in pointing out the different properties of play and their meaning for childhood development and early education, early conceptual models and theories on play and childhood development were narrowly focused. When I was introduced to play theories in my early training in child development, most of them appeared ethnocentric or rarely mentioned the cultural underpinnings of play. This tendency pervaded the psychological sciences, as the "C" word, meaning culture, was largely missing from many theoretical perspectives on play and childhood development and early education. That started to change as cultural and cross-cultural studies explored the contextual meaning of childhood socialization and development (e.g., Six Culture Studies [spearheaded by J.W.M. Whiting]). This momentum was aided by frameworks on indigenous psychology that urged the integration of epistemological knowledge from scholars in situ to extend intersubjective interpretations of the function of play. Mostly based in psychological anthropology, studies on culture and development brought to the fore the influence of the context of childhood experiences—customs, physical environment, and the ethnotheories; parental psychology, internal-working models, or cognitions of parents and teachers; about play and childhood development. Invariably, children are shaped by and shape the very nature of the play activities in which they engage in their cultural communities.

As several developmentalists have pointed out, ethnotheories guide parents' and teachers' expectations of what influences childhood development and when certain cognitive and social milestones are acquired. The incorporation of cultural dimensions into conceptual models of research on play have been far-reaching. Young children are no longer pushed to leave their culture at the doors of early childhood education centers. Efforts are increasingly being made to introduce play materials and practices that reflect children's cultural lives in their homes and communities, thus reducing discontinuity in developmental experiences between the home and early childhood education setting. This not only widens cognitive and social experiences but also enhances cultural/ethnic socialization that benefits all children—mental health, achievement, and identity. Put differently, this has lubricated inclusiveness and permitted a more serious look at the humanizing function of play—optimism and persistence in the drive to educate all children. To be clear, multidisciplinary perspectives on play have been a driving force in our understanding of pancultural and the culture-specific aspects of the developmental significance of play more broadly.

Another consideration that was introduced earlier entails risk and protective factors and childhood development. Tenets within developmental psychopathology have enabled us to discern the moderating and mediating roles of play and the quality of early childhood education on childhood development. My own work has tackled the mediating function of protective factors (e.g., parental guidance, parental cognitive engagement, preschool education) on associations between neighborhood and family risks on preschool-aged children's social and cognitive functioning in African and Caribbean cultural communities. Here, focusing more on the level and complexity of different modes of play in lessening the impact of adverse childhood experiences in the home and community (e.g., abuse, poverty, war, statelessness, climate change, neighborhood instability, and sparse educational resources) on childhood development directs thinking toward the moral ecology of playfulness and the United Nations' conception of a "World Fit for Children."

JEFF: I agree, Jaipaul, that early theories of play have been narrowly focused and ethnocentric. I feel that even some recent perspectives reflect these concerns. A good example is how play scholars and teachers now embrace the work of Lev Vygotsky. His work elevated children's play from something that is merely an enjoyable pastime to an activity that is essential to acquiring language, thought, and culturally valued knowledge and competencies. He considered culture a critical consideration in understanding play. However, he implied that a certain type of play—pretend play—was most beneficial for children. When children engage in make-believe, he argued, they think and behave as if they were "a head taller." Based on this thinking, curriculum designers and teachers have proposed models of early education in which children are guided in performing more *mature* pretend play activities. Where I live, there has been widespread adoption of the Tools of the Mind curriculum [toolsofthemind.org], in which children are provided play experiences and environments, along with adult guidance, to promote their pretend role-playing. Such approaches are found to foster deeper cognitive abilities, such as executive functions. However, this emphasis on pretend play reflects the sort of narrow, ethnocentric view you describe, Jaipaul.

When I consider Vygotsky's work, I wonder if we can really identify one universal kind of play that is valued by families of all cultures. Should pretend play, which is highly valued and frequently observed in Western cultures, be the only goal of play in classrooms? A colleague's research caused me to rethink this. She observed children in urban neighborhoods engage in active, rough play outdoors, which included the same symbolic and social benefits as play in dramatic play centers in American preschools. Other researchers have found that children in some countries and cultures are "builders" who prefer construction play to pretend role-playing—creating with blocks or even stones, sticks, or other found objects in their neighborhoods. Pretend play is important for many children around the world, but there are other forms of play that are sometimes overlooked.

Also, I wonder whether teacher involvement in children's play is always necessary or appropriate for all children. As you note, there are families in which parent-child play interactions are rare. Will children of such backgrounds feel comfortable with active teacher involvement in their play? Also, families of diverse backgrounds hold distinct cultural beliefs about the nature of adult-child relationships. In some families this relationship is formal and hierarchical; in others, it is less formal and more playful. Teachers' efforts to scaffold pretend play, as recommended by Vygotskian theorists, need to be tailored to cultural beliefs about the acceptable ways adults and children relate to one another.

JAIPAUL: Most would agree that the influence of Vygotsky's conceptions of childhood development is groundbreaking. Underlining the social contexts of children's existence and social relations within them opened the door to research on children's play in different cultural communities. Due in part to Vygotsky's thinking, relations between pretend play and language and cognitive development are well established in different research circles in the high-income countries. Pretend play is valued and encouraged in early childhood programs in these countries, where teachers provide environments that encourage rich pretend activities that move children's thinking and language to higher levels of proficiency. But as you correctly identified, Jeff, the role of pretend play in diverse cultural communities across the world is largely unknown. What and how children learn through pretend play when it occurs in diverse cultural communities remains an enigma. Nor do we know the prevalence of pretend activities in diverse cultural communities. As you discussed, in some settings the developmental significance of other forms of play may take precedent over pretend play in nurturing developmental outcomes in children. Further, in the absence of high frequencies of pretend play in some cultural communities, talk stories and telling stories can enrich children's imagination in exponential ways.

That said, as I watched children at play in northern South America recently, I cannot help but think that children's enactments of adult roles and responsibilities in cultural communities in low- and middle-income countries assist them in incorporating and adapting to the demands of life in their respective ecological niche. The Parakana Indians in Brazil enact roles that mimic adult functions, and Aka foragers in the Central African Republic engage in play activities that can be considered apprenticeships in the early mastery of skills that will lead to survival as teenagers and adults. Thus, the function of pretend and other forms of play in promoting children's cognitive and social skills may vary across cultural communities, just as rough play between fathers and children appears more common in the United States but not in several Asian and some African countries. The message here is that we need theories of play and childhood development that emerge from researchers in the communities themselves.

Turning to teacher involvement in children's play, an argument can be made that adult engagement in play with children is not as prevalent in low- and middle-income countries compared to North America and Europe. Outside of the high-income countries, parents may assume supervisory roles in play, permitting enough emotional elbow room for children to explore their object and social worlds freely on their own. Relatedly, allocaregivers—siblings and other kinship and nonkinship members—do engage in caring for and playing with children while parents are busy with economic activities. In these situations, there is a delicate balance between meeting developmental/learning goals of children and the economic needs of the family. This brings us back to your question as to whether teachers should be involved in children's play. I agree with you that this should be tailored to beliefs and cultural practices of families and the community in collaboration with educational agencies.

JEFF: Over the years, societal conditions have affected how play is viewed and supported in school. One significant development has been the inclusion of children with disabilities in regular classrooms, both in the United States and other countries. As a teacher long ago, I rarely worked with children with disabilities, since they were generally placed in self-contained special education programs. Also, children with disabilities were rarely included in my early play research, which was conducted in regular classrooms. For a time, children with more severe conditions—particularly those with autism—were believed to be unable to play. Recent research dispels this myth. All children play, but in distinct ways. Some children with intellectual disabilities engage in play that more closely resembles that of younger children, such as simple motor activity. Those with autism may prefer repetitive turn-taking games or imitative actions. Children who are hard of hearing can interact with peers in play by reading their facial clues and gestures. These are distinct forms of play. But they are, indeed, play, and are beneficial for development.

Teachers in inclusive classrooms must now adapt play materials, spaces, and interactions accordingly. To support children with disabilities, they may implement research-tested strategies—adult modeling techniques, guidance of neurotypical peers to initiate and sustain play with children who have special needs, creation of small integrated play groups within the larger classroom, or provision of augmentive communication devices. Most important, teachers must now, more than ever, base their classroom practice on careful observation and assessment of the play needs of individual children.

JAIPUAL: Inclusion and social justice are key to building a "World Fit for Children." We have made good strides in inclusive education in high-income countries, but it has remained elusive in many low- and middle-income countries. Children with disabilities are often segregated from their typical peers and stereotyped in educational settings and the community in low- and middle-income countries. Teacher training in different facets of special education is sorely lacking. Moreover, parents may have difficulties in accepting their children's disabilities due to religious and other reasons, which may interfere with their drive to attend to and advocate for children's rights and social and educational needs. On occasions, when attempts are made by teachers to provide playful learning, some services (e.g., speech and language, physical therapy) are done on a pullout rather than a push-in basis. Like you, it is my firm belief that early childhood educators are in a unique position to boost the social, motor, and cognitive skills of children with disabilities in inclusive and typical classroom settings using integrated approaches and augmented devices.

JEFF: Jaipaul, you note that preparing teachers to work with children with disabilities is lacking—particularly in low-income countries. It has been my experience in the United States that early childhood teacher preparation programs do not focus enough on young children with disabilities, generally, and methods of supporting their play, specifically. A growing body of literature indicates that various classroom play strategies are highly successful in promoting positive peer relationships by students with special needs, but implementing these requires unique teacher knowledge and abilities.

As we consider societal contexts that affect play, we must consider the explosion of technology in our world. I taught and conducted most of my research before the advent of computers and the internet, so have found technological changes dizzying. Like many professionals my age, I initially resisted technology when thinking about play. I would argue that face-to-face interactions with concrete objects were far preferable to digital games. When computers first appeared in classrooms, my mantra was: "I'd buy a set of hardwood blocks any day over a computer." Screen time was a menace, from my view, depriving children of active play or time outdoors. Digital games were abstract, passive, "electronic worksheets."

Of course, I have had to change my thinking. Technology is here to stay, for one thing, and has become a predominant way children play at home. I have heard the story—perhaps a joke—that a 5-year-old who was being read to tried to swipe a page in the book with a finger in order to turn to the next one. True or not, children have become technological beings, and we need to think of how apps can be designed to support and enhance play.

Eventually, I came to see that technology could be viewed as a powerful play material. Children play with apps with as much complexity and social interaction as when playing with dolls, Legos, or puzzles. One of my colleagues, investigating how preschool-age children program simple robots to move in desired directions, has observed children engaging in make-believe, problem-solving, and negotiation with one another as they guide these miniature creatures. Another colleague has designed an app in which children create figures with shapes—not unlike a classic set of tangrams that I provided my kindergarten students. I have observed preschoolers use a painting app on a tablet to illustrate, narrate, and enact make-believe play themes, using pretend voices of the characters they were drawing. Such activities are true play, I've come to believe.

JAIPAUL: The technological divide between the economically endowed and less economically endowed countries (also between poorly resourced and highly resourced communities in the United States) notwithstanding, technology has become an integral part and a powerful tool for engaging in different modes of play in young children's lives. You have identified numerous ways in which children use technology in play—from constructive and pretend to games. Recently, at our annual collaborative play conference among Syracuse University, The Pennsylvania State University, and The Commonwealth University of Pennsylvania held in Jamaica, we had a special session on Robots and Play. The implications for these revolutionary changes in the ecology of children's lives and for the future are mind-boggling (e.g., learning and achievement, devising future school and learning environments, social interactions, community life). At the same time, there are concerns about addiction to technology and isolation, screen time, and physical and mental health.

WHAT HAS MOST INFLUENCED YOUR THINKING OVER TIME ABOUT PLAY?

JAIPAUL: As you may have gathered throughout these exchanges, conceptual frameworks on culture and development (e.g., developmental niche, reproduction of culture, tools of the mind) and accompanying research on parenting and childhood development in diverse cultural communities have assisted in molding my thinking and research agenda on play, early education, and childhood development over the last 40 years. When I was in graduate school, there was a lacuna of developmental information on children from diverse ethnic groups in the United States and in other parts of the world. It appeared odd to me that based on work done in the Western, Educated, Industrialized, Rich Democracies (WEIRD), a small proportion of the world's population, global assertions were made about developmental phenomena and early education. Reflecting on what I was reading at the time and my own cultural upbringing, it seemed preposterous to make broad statements about childhood development based on a select body of work. Moreover, there were few, if any, courses on culture, early education, and childhood development at that time. That has improved, but we are still inclined to make many population-level generalizations when we study play, childhood development, and early education.

JEFF: I had this same experience in graduate school, Jaipaul. I recall a course on language development in which I learned the processes by which young children acquire a *single* language. It was only much later that I considered how many children around the world, and even in the United States, learn more than one language, either simultaneously or consecutively, with processes that are very different from those of monolingual children. When it came to play, I was assigned to read Piaget's work, which profiled the activities of children of European background who were often playing alone at home. It was only later that I began to think about how play might vary from Piaget's descriptions if culturally diverse families were observed, if peers or siblings were present, if toys were available at all, and if parent interactions were varied. For example, how might Piaget's profiles of his own children have differed if he or Ms. Piaget were playing with them?

JAIPAUL: Given my primary research interest in parent-child interactions (rough play, object play, affection, vocalizations, etc.), as noted already, I was intrigued by a study conducted on the Aka foragers in the Central African Republic. This study changed the trajectory of my academic career. Up to this point, I had been conducting observations of parent-child interactions in laboratory settings in which we videotaped or used small computers (SSR Keyboard) to record behaviors. The observations were then coded and analyzed. I also conducted observations of children's play and peer interactions in preschool settings. All of these observations were conducted on European American families and children in Wisconsin and Utah. As I read the descriptive accounts of parent-child interactions and investment patterns among the Aka, a people with a lengthy evolutionary past of living in the rain forest, it became abundantly clear that not only was my work narrowly focused, but the accounts of parent-child interactions, including play and parental investment patterns, were quite different from what I had observed in my early career. Moreover, I started to question the deficit models on parent-child interactions regarding diverse ethnic groups in the United Sates and other cultural groups that were floating around in academic settings. Not only were the deficit perspectives ludicrous, but they were also stereotypical. Aka fathers were very involved with their children and exceeded mothers in the display of affection and soothing behaviors toward children. These families did not engage in much rough play with children—something still highlighted as key to the development of attachment to fathers. Needless to say, this was a eureka moment for me. Thus began a journey into observing parent-child relationships and play in diverse cultural communities and in diverse ethnic groups in the United States. More recently, we have tapped into the UNICEF Micro-Indicator surveys to analyze play data in 26 African and 8 Caribbean countries. In these attempts, the goal was to further contribute to our understanding of parent-child play and cultural developmental pathways to childhood development.

JEFF: As I previously mentioned, Jaipaul, your research, which includes rich descriptions of children's play and adult-child play interactions across cultures, and that of other researchers, has greatly influenced my thinking. For example, your work on the diversity of play beliefs and interactions of fathers across cultures has caused me to rethink family contributions to children's play styles and preferences and to become more appreciative of the distinct ways children choose to play.

I also need to acknowledge the contributions to my thinking of another group of "play specialists"—3-to-5-year-olds from Puerto Rico who taught me a great deal about play by living example. I spent time interacting with preschoolers in San Juan during free play periods in their classrooms and was surprised to learn from them that play can take place anywhere and in almost any form. In elaborate music play centers created by teachers there, children would engage in complex, choreographed musical performances, pretending to be famous Latin pop stars—engaging in more make-believe than I observed when they were in their traditional dramatic play centers. I saw this same musical pretend play among children at lunchtime, when they would sing into carrots as microphones while waiting to be served. Very large groups of children in San Juan played together—once, 12 girls and boys in the blocks without any disputes and no reminders from teachers that too many people were in the center.

Another group of children—preschoolers of low English proficiency who were enrolled in a child development center at my university—demonstrated to me their impressive social and communicative strengths when playing with peers whose language they did not understand. Using gestures and facial expressions, offering objects, using peers' names or their own, these children were able to engage in remarkably elaborate play, dispelling the myth that dual-language learners necessarily have deficits in their social abilities.

So, research—my own or that of others—has been of great influence. But I have to say that it has been my expanding exposure to the play of children of diverse linguistic, cultural, and socioeconomic backgrounds that significantly shaped my thinking.

WHAT DO YOU BELIEVE MUST HAPPEN IN THE FUTURE REGARDING PLAY IN EARLY CHILDHOOD PRACTICE?

JEFF: Play in schools has become an endangered species in the United States and in other countries. First and foremost, educators and researchers must advocate for play, striving to elevate it from the relatively low status it is currently assigned in schools. Children need more, not fewer, opportunities to play—particularly in the primary grades, where school life has become very serious and teacher-directed. A powerful argument for including play in classrooms is that it supports social and emotional development, which are more predictive of long-term positive development than academic achievement.

Once play is restored to its traditional and rightful place in early education, new, more responsive play experiences and environments can be implemented in early childhood classrooms. Enhancing pretend play centers to make them more engaging and culturally relevant is only one step. A good example is a teacher of children of Navajo background who adapted her traditional dramatic play center to include more culturally relevant pretend foods and other props and to represent two apartments, rather than a single house, to create a make-believe living arrangement that was more familiar to her students. Many other types of play must also be appreciated and supported.

Musical play—more prevalent in some cultures—may be enhanced through creation of innovative classroom music centers. Active, rough outdoor play may be preferred by children of some cultures; quieter indoor games may be more appropriate for others. Space, materials, and teacher interactions can be implemented to enhance all these types of play. It is important for teachers to acquire a mindset that all culturally relevant types of play are important for development. Efforts to support play should be based on close collaboration with families—who best understand the play needs of their children—as well as careful classroom observations of individual children.

Play experiences must also be adapted for children with disabilities. Again, such efforts must be guided by collaborations with families and based on classroom observations. One teacher learned from a parent that a student with autism enjoyed turn-taking activities—engaging more with others when participating in imitation games with peers. Another teacher observed that a student with an intellectual disability engaged in repetitive motor actions and very simple pretense. In both cases, teachers successfully encouraged and enhanced these types of play in classrooms.

The role of teachers and peers in play should be refined and elaborated. Specific teacher strategies to scaffold play in responsive, unobtrusive, and respectful ways should be designed and tested. A method in which neurotypical peers are guided in supporting play of those with disabilities holds promise. Teacher efforts to promote play and its associated social and emotional development require knowledge and skill. Coursework and field experiences related to play, culture, and disabilities should be required in early childhood teacher education.

JAIPAUL: I totally agree with you, Jeff, that far more emphasis should be placed on play in classroom settings, with considerations of children's cultural backgrounds and preferences for different modes of play. Equally important is the need to further build on education practices and the role of play in advancing social development and peer relations in inclusive settings with appropriate materials (ELL, children with disabilities, trauma, statelessness, etc.). I would like to add to the cogent points you made by calling further attention to the need to carefully document the wide array of play activities that children engage in across cultures and their significance for designing programs for children in indoor and outdoor spaces in different cultural communities. In my opinion, play is narrowly defined, and classrooms miss activities that may be considered playful in other cultural communities. In this vein, there is a growing emphasis on nature play and corresponding interest in constructing outdoor play spaces that are developmentally appropriate. Finally, we need to construct more indigenous conceptual frameworks on play and early education, develop culturally sensitive assessment tools that emerge from the cultures themselves and not simply modify existing tools to fit the culture, and build early childhood education programs that incorporate the input of community members and children. Movement in these directions would most certainly assist in decolonizing our minds about play, early education, and childhood development; advance the rights of children; and build a more just and sustainable world that is "Fit for Children."

Reflections on the Place of Play in Early Childhood Education Conversation

Nancy File

Play is a topic so extensively associated with the field of early childhood education throughout its history that it was a given in our table of contents as we planned this project. Perhaps some things about play seem self-evident; it would be surprising to find a reader with no personal experience with play. Play is what we in the field believe that young children should be doing in programs, and many would say we know play when we see it. Yet the contributors for this chapter have given us much to consider regarding more nuanced and complex understandings of what play can be and what it means to children and society.

Early in the conversation, Jaipaul and Jeff establish the place of play in children's lives, declaring that children "must" play and "need" to play. Their vivid childhood memories illuminate how meaningful play was to their childhood selves. As they come to the close of their conversation, they both advocate for a stronger place for play in classrooms in the future. For decades, there has been much concern about the pushdown of content and teaching practices from older classrooms to younger ones. These concerns are supported by research showing that teachers' practices and expectations of children have shifted, with kindergarten now resembling the 1st grade of the previous decades. As children have been pushed to demonstrate more academic learning earlier, the time available for play has decreased, "learning centers" are becoming more common than "playtime," and the teacher's curricular agenda has exerted more influence. This is a trend that Jeff and Jaipaul have laid out steps to counter, an important contribution of their conversation.

Both Jaipaul and Jeff discuss a focus on early academics. Jaipaul described the "academic training" emphasis that he has observed in classrooms in many different countries. Jeff explained the emphasis on school readiness in the United States. This phenomenon has pushed teachers to justify play by joining it to academic goals, ensuring that play opportunities come paired with learning points. It carries the potential to reduce children's opportunities to direct their own experiences. Jeff mentioned guided play, in which the teacher has an agenda for children's learning but utilizes playful means to draw upon children's inclinations and engagement levels in play. While certainly a teaching strategy much more aligned with young children's nature than drills and worksheets, we must consider whether children in our classrooms are granted agency to try out their own ideas, form their own plans, and act upon materials and their world as they desire. Is there a mix of forms of play and playful learning activities or guided play that we believe is best to provide for young children? Is it possible to expect a consensus answer for "we" as a field, or are wide differences in the experiences children might have a natural by-product of a field provided in different auspices and with varied forms of control from federal, state, and/or local levels?

It is a long way from the 1950s and 1960s, when children's first encounters with group programs likely happened in kindergarten or first grade. As ever-younger children began to participate in early childhood settings, how the missions of care and education were realized has been both varied at any one time and shifting over time. Today, in a prekindergarten program conducted within the public school, it is not unusual to see reference to the "literacy block." Some programs promote a reputation for play, others for more directed teaching and learning. Many different stakeholders are involved in determining what happens in classrooms for young children. For readers, the vital question is, what is important for the life spaces occupied by young children? If play is what young children must do (even into the primary-grade years), as asserted within the conversation, what will it take to ensure that they have opportunities to live lives that allow them rich play opportunities?

One striking feature of this conversation was the discussion Jaipaul and Jeff offered about the importance they place upon diversity. Jaipaul's interests in international research emerged early in his career. Jeff modeled a typical pattern within the field of early childhood for those of us native to the United States and belonging to the dominant culture, a realization over time that diverse experiences and perspectives had been missing. Both are strong advocates for supporting play through a lens of cultural and linguistic diversity, but also in light of developmental diversity and meeting the play styles of children with disabilities. Because play emerges from children's lives, it is much more than each of us has known individually. Clearly, to introduce diversity as a feature of one's understanding of and stance toward play will create the need for much deeper and more complex thinking about the work of a teacher. With greater attention paid to these understandings over time, teacher preparation is now much different from what Jeff experienced as he (and those of his generation) entered the field. Still, it is important to continue the efforts in this vein to ensure that play opportunities support all children and reflect the communities in which they live.

The belief in play evidenced in the conversation was linked by both Jeff and Jaipaul to its benefits, particularly for children's social and emotional development. Frequently in the United States children who are viewed as "being behind" their peers, children of color and/or living in poverty, are offered more academic content in a belief that this will change the trajectory of their learning. Jaipaul was clear that the disparities he has seen among nations are evident as well within the United States in regard to income groups. He raises an interesting consideration in his research about play as a protective factor in children's development. That is, is play particularly valuable for children who are living in poverty, experiencing food insecurity and instability, and/or facing various forms of upheaval? Where does play figure in giving children the best chances to experience satisfying lives?

Jaipaul referred to the "humanizing function" of play and the vision of a "World Fit for Children." The latter phrase comes from a declaration passed by the United Nations (UN) in 2002. This declaration followed the UN Convention on the Rights of the Child, adopted in 1989. The Convention declared children's right to play, among other things, including broad attention to factors that challenge or support children as they grow toward adulthood. It has been ratified by every country except for the United States. The 2002 declaration "A World Fit for Children" was intended to further define steps forward in this broadly based vision, which includes attention to health, economics, and schooling, among other factors. Within the World Fit for Children declaration, there is an affirmation that children should experience respect, dignity, security, and well-being. There is a stated intent that they should enjoy childhood, a "time of play and learning." Readers interested in learning more can access the document through the list of further readings. It seems appropriate to end on this note, a realization of how important childhood is, what it is that children need and deserve, and how play figures within this perspective. Jeff and Jaipaul point us toward considerations of how conversations about play are structured around profound ideas—play is anything but frivolous or commonsense. How can we preserve its place in the lives of young children?

QUESTIONS FOR DISCUSSION

1. The contributors of this dialogue believe that play is essential for young children. Should it be considered a right for children? If so, might anything change in American society?
2. Jaipaul and Jeff described several different theoretical approaches to play. What is the potential impact of changing how we think about play?
3. How important is child agency in play? What does this mean for teachers of young children?

FOR FURTHER READING

California Department of Education. (2021). *The powerful role of play in early education.* cde.ca.gov/sp/cd/re/documents/powerfulroleofplay.pdf

General Assembly Resolution S-27/2. *A world fit for children,* A/RES/S-27/2. (10 May 2002). https://documents-dds-ny.un.org/doc/UNDOC/GEN/N02/481/78/PDF/N0248178.pdf?OpenElement

Johnson, J. E., & Wu, V. M-H. (2019). Perspectives on play in early childhood care and education. In C. P. Brown, M. B. McMullen, & N. File (Eds.), *The Wiley handbook of early childhood care and education* (pp. 79–97). John Wiley & Sons.

Lynch, M. (2015). More play, please: The perspective of kindergarten teachers on play in the classroom. *American Journal of Play, 7,* 347–370.

Pyle, A., & Bigelow, A. (2015). Play in kindergarten: An interview and observational study in three Canadian classrooms. *Early Childhood Education Journal, 43,* 385–393.

Roopnarine, J. L., & Davidson, K. L. (2015). Parent-child play across cultures: Advancing play research. *American Journal of Play,* 7, 228–252.

Smith, P., & Roopnarine, J. L. (Eds.). (2019). *The Cambridge handbook on play: Developmental and disciplinary perspectives.* Cambridge University Press.

Trawick-Smith, J. (2010). Drawing back the lens on play: A frame analysis of young children's play in Puerto Rico. *Early Education and Development, 21,* 536–567.

Trawick-Smith, J. (2022). *Young children's play: Development, disabilities, and diversity.* Routledge.

CHAPTER 5

Curriculum and Pedagogy in Early Childhood Education

J. Amos Hatch and Marjorie Kostelnik

J. **Amos Hatch** is professor emeritus at the University of Tennessee. He began his career teaching K–3 children in urban elementary schools in Kansas City, Missouri, and Jacksonville, Florida. After earning his Ph.D., he shifted to teaching teachers and advanced graduate students at The Ohio State University and the University of Tennessee. To date, Amos has published nine books, authored over 150 journal articles and book chapters, and presented scores of papers at academic conferences around the globe. His published work has been translated into Spanish, Chinese, and Korean. He was executive editor of two important education journals, served in leadership capacities in multiple professional organizations, and was the recipient of numerous awards for teaching, scholarship, and professional service. Although retired, he continues to think and write about critical issues in early childhood education and beyond. His latest book is *Teaching as a Human Activity: Ways to Make Classrooms Joyful and Effective.*

Dr. **Marjorie Kostelnik** is professor emeritus and inaugural dean of the College of Education and Human Sciences at the University of Nebraska, Lincoln. Previously, during 2 decades at Michigan State, she taught ECE courses and served as program supervisor of the Child Development Laboratories and as department chair of Family and Child Ecology. During 22 years at UNL, besides administrative duties, Marjorie taught classes in early childhood methods. She was co-leader of the Prosper Lincoln early childhood initiative and co-chair of the Nebraska Early Childhood Workforce Commission. Nationally, Marjorie served as vice president of NAEYC and as a member of the National Academies of Science Institute of Medicine Committee to Study the Science of Children Birth to Age 8. During her career, Marjorie worked with 120-plus community and higher education programs in the United States and internationally, exploring implications of developmentally appropriate practices for ECE-related instruction of children, teachers, and administrators.

AT THE START OF YOUR CAREER, WHAT WERE THE PREVALENT INFLUENCES ON ECE CURRICULUM AND TEACHING/PEDAGOGY?

AMOS: My first experiences with early childhood programs were as an undergrad student at the University of Utah volunteering at a Head Start center in Salt Lake City. It was the early 1970s, I had just gotten out of the army, and I was a rising junior studying political science. I took a summer course that visited various service-related sites in the area, and I fell in love with the program (especially its emphasis on families and meeting the needs of the whole child) and the people (especially the young children) at the Head Start center. Working nights in a warehouse and going to school full-time, I still found time to volunteer two or three mornings a week at the center. I decided I wanted to be a Head Start teacher.

When I went to my advisors at the university to see about an early childhood degree, I learned that it would add almost 2 years to complete a program in what was then the College of Home Economics. However, the College of Education could get me a degree and teaching license without adding too much time, so I took that route. My teacher education program was unapologetically based in the progressive tenets of the day (e.g., the goal of education ought to be to enable children to become self-fulfilled; teachers should be facilitators of children's experiences; children will not learn until their physical, safety, belonging, and self-esteem needs are met). We read all the radical educators—from Carl Rogers to A. S. Neill. I bought into these ideas and thought working with young kids who were growing up in economic circumstances like I experienced as a child would make me a soldier in the war on poverty.

MARJORIE: Amos, I'm struck by your determination to make a difference in children's lives and your pursuit of that goal from the start. I, too, wanted to have an impact but was unsure of how; I tried a different major every semester for 2 years. Then in 1970, the University of Pittsburgh announced a new program—child development. It addressed young children's development and learning as well as mental health interventions. We read Erikson,

Axline, Bettelheim, Piaget, and Read. Students participated in four part-time practicums and two full-time internships, enabling me to experience the remarkable range of the field (e.g., preschool, child care, residential treatment, Head Start, supporting children with learning disabilities). I felt unlimited in my options for enhancing children's lives.

After graduation, I spent 2 years as a lead teacher in an urban child care center. The work was eye-opening, exhausting, and exhilarating. To learn more, I enrolled in graduate studies in Human Development and Family Studies at Penn State. There I entered a new world of theory and practice. As an undergraduate, I had assumed I was learning the "child development way." At Penn State, I discovered there were many approaches to early childhood education based on differing theories. Three of these were modeled and studied in the lab school. There was a Behavioral classroom, a Piagetian classroom, and a Social-Emotional classroom applying the practices of Carl Rogers and Louise Guerney. I became a teacher in the Social-Emotional model. At the time, there was significant competition among ECE models nationally, with researchers hoping to find the "best" ones to disseminate nationwide.

Simultaneously, a hallmark [1972] article by Reese and Overton posited that certain metatheories represented incompatible worldviews about human development and learning. One had to choose a single metatheory and reject others in order to achieve content validity within proposed interventions. Thus, in our graduate studies we were encouraged to explore both mechanistic and organismic theories and practices, but then to choose only one to follow in our own approaches to ECE.

AMOS: It's interesting that you would point to Reese and Overton's notion of selecting a theoretical orientation and then sticking with it. My view is that that kind of thinking persists in ECE, so we take sides and label practices as good or bad, right or wrong, appropriate or inappropriate. As my classroom career got under way, I was too naïve or too idealistic to think deeply about potential theoretical conflicts related to my teaching. I never became a Head Start teacher. After graduation, I moved to Kansas City, Missouri, and took a job as a 2nd-grade teacher in a segregated elementary school housing a Project Follow Through "Behavior Analysis" program run by Kansas University. At that time, the Head Start program in Kansas City was not up to the quality I observed in Salt Lake, so I took the Follow Through job.

As you point out, the 1970s were a time when lots of resources and effort were spent trying to find the best educational practices for children who were considered "disadvantaged." Some studies indicated that the positive initial effects of Head Start faded out when kids entered the primary grades, and Project Follow Through was set up to award grants for designing and testing programs that *followed through* on the early learning gains from Head Start. Different programs were based on different philosophies and theories. My program applied behaviorism to the max. We had a token economy, and the day was divided between earn and spend times. We had programmed materials that were set up to encourage students to respond to prompts. The adults (three parent assistants and I) passed out soft plastic tokens when children responded correctly. At some level I knew that teaching in this behaviorist program flew in the face of what I had learned in my teacher prep program, but it didn't trouble me. I loved this school, made wonderful connections with children and families (I moved into the community in which I taught), and felt like I was doing meaningful work.

MARJORIE: It sounds like you had a rewarding experience as a beginning teacher. You were in a "model" program working with children every day using research-based practices. Such models offered chances to examine different approaches and to envision new ways of teaching. I believe ECE benefited from these efforts. Your statement that the emphasis on competing metatheories within education had some negative fallout mirrors my experiences, too. As you noted, most damaging was the idea that competing perspectives were either right or wrong. Yet, your personal experience in Project Follow Through illustrated that applied behaviorism could be effective in reaching specific goals; my experiences in the social-emotional preschool demonstrated the benefit of strategies associated with emotional awareness.

In my opinion, the metatheory dichotomy had important points to make regarding program integrity but got in the way of identifying universal high-quality practices we could all agree on regardless of model. That is why I was intrigued to learn that other fields, such as public administration, viewed mechanistic and organismic approaches to program design as part of a continuum rather than a dichotomy. The two points of the continuum were neither good nor bad, just better-suited or less well suited to address particular situations and challenges. This pedagogical "aha" has influenced my teaching practices and curriculum beliefs ever since.

AMOS: I like continuums, too. I've used them in my teaching and writing to try to help students and readers think more broadly about decision-making related to curriculum and pedagogy. Looks like we share a commitment to preparing teachers to make sound decisions about what to teach and how to teach based on a complex set of professional skills, understandings, and dispositions.

Returning to the question that frames this part of our discussion, the prevalent influences on ECE curriculum and teaching/pedagogy at the start of my career included some we have mentioned and others that are related but not named (e.g., HighScope, Montessori, Waldorf). My overall impression of the early childhood field in the 1970s was that there were ongoing tensions around "developmental" versus "academic" programs, "play-based" versus "structured" approaches, "child-initiated" versus "teacher-directed" activities, and "child care" versus "education" focuses. During this time, I moved to Jacksonville, Florida, took a job teaching primary-age children in a newly desegregated urban elementary school, and completed a master's degree at night at University of North Florida. Again, there was dissonance between what I was learning in my early childhood coursework and what I was doing in my classroom. Marjorie, it sounds like your experience at Penn State gave you some powerful tools for thinking through relationships among metatheories and what that means for curriculum and teaching in ECE. Looking back, it seems like I was so focused on what was right in front of me that I didn't step back and take in the bigger picture.

MARJORIE: Of course, what was in front of you was what counts most: children. Your big picture was each classroom in which you taught, and your work experiences bridged the worlds of theory to practice. The disconnect between what you learned in your coursework and strategies enacted in schools illustrates the "dichotomies" we underwent. Thus, the pedagogical metatheory divides were more than hypothetical dilemmas; we each experienced them firsthand. In addition, the mutually exclusive positions of "this versus that" that you highlighted about teaching strategies and philosophies all resonate with me. I remember heated conversations about such issues in the programs in which I taught, among my colleagues in different ECE settings, and in professional meetings. In fact, one's teaching approach was sometimes treated as a moral choice versus an intellectual one. All of this illustrates the cognitive and emotional dissonance many experienced as the field endeavored to define "good teaching."

Although this churn was challenging to navigate, there were benefits, too. Differing approaches encouraged us to think in new ways and to reorganize or expand ideas about goals, strategies, and outcomes in ECE. Greater attention was focused on children from diverse backgrounds and those with differing abilities. Instructional experimentation and program evaluation accelerated. This intense scrutiny contributed to early childhood programs being perceived as having the potential to do much more than simply "keep children busy and safe." Consequently, public policy became a bigger part of the picture also. Although I didn't know it then, these early days signaled a new era for ECE in terms of mission and practices.

HOW HAVE THESE INFLUENCES CHANGED OVER YOUR CAREER?

MARJORIE: After completing my doctorate, I became a faculty member at Michigan State. I taught classes in ECE, became director of the Child Development Laboratories (serving 200 children, infants through kindergarten), and eventually became department chair. All of these roles gave me opportunities to work directly with aspiring educators, practitioners on the job, researchers, policymakers, children, and families. Over the years I observed that the philosophical conversations across the field became increasingly informed by research and evaluation. Some questions we asked included:

- What educational benefits can we expect from early childhood programs?
- Who are the children and families being served and what are their needs?
- Where should program content originate?
- Are certain curricula or instructional strategies "best," and if so, for whom?
- Where do family members fit into the educational process?

The search for answers to queries like these ultimately influenced teaching practices. To secure better answers, we expanded our research and evaluative procedures to encompass a wider range of methods and instrumentation. In addition, we gradually moved from seeking single solutions to developing a wider array of approaches. Most importantly, we became ecosystemic in our work, recognizing the interactive impacts of families, the workforce itself, community members, stakeholders, and policymakers in how they influenced children's development and learning.

Significantly, early childhood attracted increasing attention and scrutiny from scholars outside its traditional boundaries. Today, neuroscientists and economists as well as business and public policy specialists carry out work that contributes to our understanding of ECE. All of this bodes well—yet we still have mountains to climb in terms of ECE affordability, the status of the early childhood workforce, and those stubborn either/or mentalities that linger.

AMOS: I support your assessment about how traditional boundaries have been stretched over the course of the past 40 years and agree that we have more mountains to climb in ECE. As I consider how curriculum and teaching have changed during my career, my mind runs to events and experiences that altered my own thinking. During the 1980s, I started my doctoral program at the University of Florida while I was still teaching in Jacksonville. I took sabbatical leave from my teaching to finish my coursework, but then owed 2 years back to the system. The first year back I worked with the district-wide primary education program; the second, I taught kindergarten.

I was still in graduate school when *A Nation at Risk* was published. The 1983 report warned that schools were failing to educate students adequately; that the nation's future was at risk; and that increased rigor, higher standards, and more testing were needed to avoid disaster. The themes of this report have shaped education reform efforts ever since. For ECE, in particular, the reform movement generated lots of pressure to push curriculum down, to limit time for play and exploration, and to assess student progress against rigorous standards.

The publication of the original *Developmentally Appropriate Practices* handbook in 1987 was another landmark moment for me. I had been teaching early childhood courses at Ohio State University's Marion campus for a couple of years when "the green bible" came out. For me, it was the perfect counter to the radical reform narrative of *A Nation at Risk*. I was a true believer and I preached from the handbook, even when I saw experienced educators in my graduate classes weep when they saw that how they were teaching was identified as "developmentally inappropriate practice." I'll talk about how my relationship with DAP has changed below, but these two landmark publications show the impact of some of the competing influences of the 1980s.

MARJORIE: The two publications you cited were groundbreaking, and I can see why you chose them as touchpoints. They exemplify key notions that have influenced the field through today. Of course, as you state, they also represented conflicting ideas about how to move early education forward.

In terms of my own career, after more than 20 years of being engaged in ECE, life changed for me. I was elected to the NAEYC Governing Board in 1994 and in 2000 I moved again, this time to the University of Nebraska, Lincoln (UNL), where I became dean of the College of Human Resources and Family Sciences (HRFS). Both experiences gave me a chance to see ECE in new ways.

Being on the NAEYC board gave me a stronger national perspective. Through in-person meetings with members nationwide, I experienced the passion practitioners had for their work with young children, as well as their desire to provide the highest-quality services possible. I also became more aware of how challenging that was due to lack of resources, fissures in the field among program types, difficulty accessing training, and lack of respect for ECE work from policymakers. I was aware of these challenges in my previous roles, but their pervasive nature and national import really hit home for me now.

Within 3 years of my arrival on campus I found myself in the midst of creating a new college, the College of Education and Human Sciences (CEHS). Members of two colleges, Teachers College and HRFS, voted to join together as a single entity. The aim was to develop more interdisciplinary ways of approaching education and other human interventions. This effort brought together in one college a critical mass of professions engaged in serving young children. It was an opportunity to create new approaches to bridging some of the divides that had traditionally existed among differing early childhood majors—it was exciting!

AMOS: It's interesting to compare how our careers unfolded. I moved from Ohio State to the University of Tennessee, where I spent the next 30 years as a professor. Dramatic influences changed my point of view during the first half of that tenure. Two events symbolize the complexity of those influences: (a) a conference I organized in 1989 on qualitative research in ECE and (b) (like you) my election to the NAEYC Governing Board. The conference happened because I was invited to edit a special edition of *Qualitative Studies in Education (QSE)*, and my dean supported bringing in top scholars in this relatively new field. The attendees were so stimulated by the conference that they wanted to meet again, which led to the formation of the Reconceptualizing Early Childhood Education (RECE) group. My election to the NAEYC board was a shock. Some sitting board members heard me speak, nominated me, and supported my candidacy.

I attended the first RECE meeting and have been to 20 or so over the years. At first, I came looking for articles for *QSE*, having become executive editor in 1991. Soon I started doing papers and participating more actively. From RECE colleagues, I learned to be much more critical as I thought about ECE theory, research, policy, and practice. This group was especially critical of DAP, NAEYC, and the ECE establishment. I was among the most conservative participants, but my new perspectives led me to organize debates and discussions about DAP at NAEYC conferences and other venues. On the other hand, I was considered a radical on the NAEYC board. Like you, Marjorie, my 4-year service on the board was profound—the most powerful professional development experience of my career. In both settings, I saw the need for change and tried to work *within* RECE and NAEYC to make a difference.

MARJORIE: Just as in your work with RECE and NAEYC, I believe changes in ECE-related academic programs and pedagogy are best served via "inside" processes. In creating CEHS, many faculty, students, and alumni wanted to contribute to improving the lives of young children, families, and practitioners. Although this focus was addressed by people in some programs previously, that was not so collegewide. Also, working toward greater integration of ECE content across colleges had not been traditional, and the historic pedagogical dichotomies you identified earlier were clearly operating here. Following much discussion, ECE became a "new-college" priority. Agreements were made to work collectively versus unilaterally in certain arenas, respecting differences of opinion and scholarly ideas. It was not a one-size-fits-all effort. Many strategies were employed to achieve a common sense of purpose. For example, interest groups were formed around certain questions and seed money was provided to support teaching or research that traversed department or philosophical boundaries. Although this work began almost 20 years ago, it undergoes continuous review and modification to address current needs and accommodate newcomers. As a result, the focus on young children across CEHS has been maintained and honed through the administrations of three deans, changes in internal structures, and the fiscal ups and downs typical in public institutions today. In fact, the emphasis on young children is one of the strongest themes undergirding the interdisciplinary teaching, research, and outreach within CEHS and, more recently, the University of Nebraska system.

AMOS: It's amazing what you were able to accomplish in bringing different folks with different ideas together around a common purpose. It seems to me that that approach should be a model for higher education and our field. Thinking about how influences have changed, my own career has taken me from being a DAP disciple to arguing that the field has placed too much emphasis on development and not enough on learning. Thinking about our discussion, I went back to two letters I wrote to DAP editors when revisions were in progress. In the 1992 letter, I called for less either/or thinking and more continuums (citing one of your publications, Marjorie); more attention to "individual appropriateness"; a broader take on ECE theory and research; and more attention to the social contexts of education. By 2007, I was suggesting that the term "developmentally appropriate practice" be abandoned; subject matter and teaching should get much more attention; more emphasis should be placed on teacher decision-making; and the knowledge base on which the handbook was based should go beyond its overemphasis on Piaget-based developmental psychology. I was invited but did not take the opportunity to provide input on the 2020 DAP position statement revision. It's interesting to look at how reactions to my published work have changed over the years from hero for defending educators' rights to implement developmental approaches to heretic for throwing DAP under the bus.

WHAT HAS BEEN GAINED AND LOST BECAUSE OF THESE CHANGES?

AMOS: Looking at the latest version of the DAP handbook, it seems to me that there have been gains regarding some of the issues we have been talking about. Compared to earlier editions, there is more space given to the learning side of the "development and learning" divide in the 2022 volume. Further, there is increased attention to subject-matter curricula and more latitude given to teacher-directed activity. I know the texts you have published on implementing DAP have had a positive influence in moving the needle in these directions, and I think this is a plus for the field at large. I know that NAEYC is not the only arbiter of what counts as appropriate subject matter and pedagogy in ECE, but, as I will argue later, I don't think DAP or the field has come far enough in many areas (including curriculum and teaching).

As an NAEYC board member and as a teacher and scholar, one of my goals was to question the assumptions that folks use as a basis for their points of view. I applied this approach when critiquing both sides of the conservative/radical divide. When explaining my stance on debunking assumptions to a colleague at a Reconceptualizing ECE conference in Australia, her response was, "Oh, you're just a curmudgeon." Explaining my rationale to NAEYC associates, I said things like, "You stop thinking when you don't take a close look at what you are taking for granted." I have been intentionally provocative in an effort to provoke deeper thought about the complex issues that confront us. In terms of ECE curriculum and pedagogy, I have called for a much clearer delineation of what should be taught and a much broader conceptualization of how it should be taught. I don't see that clarity or breadth in the latest DAP guidelines.

MARJORIE: Your observations illustrate how difficult it is to address differing pedagogical beliefs in ECE, even among people of good will. We are still divided in some of our fundamental interpretations of what constitutes effective teaching practices. Your concerns about the latest DAP document illustrate this dilemma.

However, when I compare my first job as a child care teacher with the ECE students we are educating today, I see a huge difference in their preparation and in the ECE settings they are experiencing—including child care, preschool, special education, and early elementary. In my first classroom, I had 25 children, a predetermined schedule, and a classroom that had to be set up and taken down daily. What we didn't have was a curriculum to follow, program goals, ways to evaluate impact, or opportunities to meet with parents. There was no inservice training, and planning time was 1 hour per week. This was a highly touted community program, one of which supervisors and families were proud. So you see, from my vantage point, the field has come a long way since 1974. We have gained a deeper body of knowledge and a wider array of experts whose work informs ECE. Consequently, we have become more nuanced in our approaches and have held ourselves to more stringent standards in developing conclusions. Most importantly, the knowledge base has become more inclusive and more diverse in terms of the scholars and practitioners whose work addresses teaching practices and ECE evaluation methods. From these changes we've gained:

- stronger links between theory, research, and practice;
- more reliable, inclusive data on effective teaching strategies;

- greater attention to learning across the entire age span, birth to 8;
- a broader array of effective teaching practices;
- more options for program design; and
- stronger methods of program evaluation.

Each of these factors has strengthened the field through improved teaching strategies and more relevant curricula. However, the work isn't finished.

AMOS: Your list of gains is impressive and, it seems to me, right on target. The third question asks for what's been gained and lost over the course of our careers, and it's hard to come up with anything related to ECE curriculum and teaching/pedagogy that I would count as a net loss. We have moved forward for sure, but as you note, there's always more to do.

One area in which I think our field has missed the opportunity to do more is the upper age range of early childhood. When I was on the NAEYC board, I pushed for more attention to the realities of teaching and learning in K–3 programs. I pointed out the small number of kindergarten and (especially) primary- grade teachers who chose to join the organization, the dearth of K–3-focused sessions at conferences and articles in NAEYC journals, and what I saw as the disconnect between what the organization was telling teachers was "appropriate" and what was actually going on in schoolrooms for children ages 5 through 8. Trying to provoke some serious consideration of the issues involved, I proposed that NAEYC drop the primary grades and focus on programs for children from birth through kindergarten age. I tried to disrupt the assumption that pedagogy and curriculum designed for very young children were also a perfect fit for young school-age kids. Of course, that idea had all the energy of a lead balloon. We talked about doing more for K–3 teachers, but not much really changed.

My tenure on the board ended in 2002, so there has been time for ECE as a field to acknowledge and address differences across the birth-to-8 age span. Again, we have done better, but I still think this area represents a lost opportunity to do more. I want to be clear that I have argued strenuously that much of what goes on in public education is misguided and sometimes harmful (e.g., the implementation of "teacher-proof" curriculums and the imposition of standards-based accountability regimes). My point is that ECE as a field has not found effective tools for articulating differences in how children's capacities, education contexts, and societal expectations change across what we consider "early childhood."

MARJORIE: I agree that there are ongoing gaps in our efforts to address the needs of children and teachers in all ECE classrooms. Lack of involvement by K–3 teachers in NAEYC is a telling illustration of this challenge. That example also underscores fragmentation within the field. Although we are striving for greater coherence, we remain divided in many ways (e.g., setting, ages of children served, metatheory foundations, and funding sources, to name a few). This fragmentation impedes activities like recruiting new members to the profession or seeking public policy support for ECE. Although there are many reasons for such challenges, we in higher education cannot ignore our contributions to the dilemma. Most importantly, we have not been very successful in bridging the theoretical and pedagogical divides among the disciplines that address ECE in our institutions.

Because the early childhood workforce involves different ECE-related majors, academic preparation in each one is often siloed within disparate programs on campus. Thus, aspiring child care teachers, elementary teachers, and early childhood special education majors are typically educated in relatively self-contained programs, departments, and/or colleges. Each of these specialties has its own:

- age ranges of children served;
- history in the field;
- history at the institution;
- preferred metatheories;
- paths to graduation;
- pedagogical traditions;
- practica;
- professional organizations;
- academic requirements;
- research base;
- revered figures/experts; and
- vocabulary.

Consequently, variations among ECE programs are difficult to navigate. And, as you learned when you made your own initial inquiries about potential ECE majors, program requirements vary in prerequisites, acceptance of transfer credits, and so on. All of these circumstances segregate ECE programs rather than promote coherence and collaboration among them. Thus, on campus, it's not uncommon for students to remain fixed in their particular academic homes, seldom crossing ECE boundaries, sharing experiences, or exploring classroom practices beyond their specialties. Yet once those graduates get into the community, they may all be working with the same children and families, sometimes on the same team, sometimes on their own, and sometimes in actual conflict with one another's methods. This state of affairs is counterproductive for students and for ECE.

AMOS: Yes, universities as institutions are famous for building academic barriers that separate faculty into silos, and ECE is a prime example of how those barriers compartmentalize the experience of students and impact their preparation for operating in the real world. My tenure in higher education included aspects of each of the elements on your list. In my own experience, state teacher licensure was another confounding dimension that led to lots of confusion and sometimes to conflict across academic departments. To make things worse, the state of Tennessee could not make up its mind about how to structure ECE licensure, so who could offer what license to which students was a moving target. Including early childhood special education licensure made things even more complex and (sometimes) contentious.

In my state and many others, state legislatures, departments of education, governors' offices, and school boards are currently placing new restrictions on what is taught and how from preschool through graduate education. I take up these additional challenges as we discuss the future of ECE curriculum and pedagogy/teaching in the next question.

MARJORIE: Many of our ECE colleagues will identify with your observations. Those examples underscore why teaching practices are often inconsistent across academic programs and ECE community settings. Of course, we are not the first to recognize such challenges. The splintered nature of the field regarding curriculum and pedagogy has long been a subject of consternation and deliberation. Most recently, the Institute of Medicine and the National Research Council (IOM/NRC) convened a nationwide committee of ECE teachers, researchers, administrators, and policymakers to address ways to transform the ECE workforce by creating a unifying scientific foundation for the field. I was fortunate to serve on this committee. One of the many issues that surfaced was lack of common training and contact among *all* early childhood students across majors within the same and different institutions prior to graduating. This was viewed as a barrier to enhancing ECE pedagogy. Among the task force's recommendations, committee members were challenged to become problem-solvers and change agents within our own organizations/campuses. That charge has shaped my vision of the future.

WHAT DO YOU SEE AS THE PRIMARY PURPOSE OF ECE, AND WHAT SHOULD CURRICULUM AND TEACHING/PEDAGOGY LOOK LIKE IN THE FUTURE?

MARJORIE: I believe the ultimate aim of ECE is to enhance the lives of all young children, birth through age 8, by providing high-quality programs that support holistic development and learning. There's a lot that goes into this purpose to make it reality, but that's it in a nutshell. Going back to our observations earlier in this chapter, this aim cannot be achieved without access to a well-educated workforce. By "well-educated," I'm not referring to any particular degree, certificate, or major. I am talking about a workforce that has the knowledge and skills it needs to achieve the ECE purpose. Such a workforce would value itself and be valued by others in esteem, in remuneration, in community pride, and in public policy support.

Moreover, when we talk about curriculum and teaching, we are addressing two layers of application: the teaching that happens in ECE programs with children and the instruction that guides the preparation of their teachers. To achieve high-quality outcomes in both arenas, I would go back to the IOM/NRC report. Two of its 12 recommendations have particular relevance to the question posed here. These are for higher education (ranging from community colleges through graduate school) to:

- Build an interdisciplinary foundation of shared knowledge and competencies for the academic preparation of *all* early childhood professionals regardless of their home discipline.
- Support consistent quality and coherence of professional learning across roles, groups, and settings for *all* early childhood teachers in training regardless of specific major.

These ideas set the stage for developing future agendas to take us beyond our current state of affairs.

AMOS: Sounds like the work of your committee is an important step in raising the value of ECE in the eyes of those inside and outside the profession. Having a recognized knowledge base and preparing future teachers to understand and apply it would be a big advance toward increasing the respect ECE deserves.

I think your nutshell definition of the purposes of ECE is right on target. I have argued throughout my career that having a shared purpose is key to providing meaningful experiences across the education spectrum. Improving the life chances of all children has been the driving aim at the core of my thinking, teaching, writing, and service activity since I entered the ECE field. It would be great if all the stakeholders (i.e., teachers, administrators, students, parents, communities, legislators, policymakers, and scholars) could agree on a purpose and frame everything they do so that that purpose was accomplished, but often, agreement is hard to find.

As I foreshadowed earlier in our dialogue, the political discourse in states like Tennessee has become infected with accusations that education institutions are indoctrinating students with "liberal" values and turning them away from loving their country. Educators are seen as part of a "woke mob" that makes majority children feel guilty for the imaginary sins of their ancestors. Ultraconservative state legislatures and local school boards are passing legislation and enacting rules that impact how future ECE teachers are prepared, what materials (including children's books) can be included in classrooms and libraries, what history can be taught, and even what methods teachers can apply. ECE has a strong history of working to enhance the lives of *all* young children (e.g., anti-bias education, culturally appropriate practice). That stance is being challenged by powerful forces that have other purposes in mind.

MARJORIE: Your observations regarding our current culture wars are insightful, raising concerns we can't ignore. As you noted, agreements around teaching and curriculum can be hard to come by for numerous reasons. Yet, like you, I believe we need to keep pursuing stronger ties across the field. I've learned that this work is most successful when it is relationship-based and deliberate. For example, it wasn't enough to simply "put" early care and development, special education, and elementary education in the same college, hoping that proximity would guarantee interaction and collaboration. Naturally, there were task forces and committees to explore possibilities. However, it was relationship-building, willingness to take risks, and recognizing that "great" ideas could not succeed without great effort that prompted new alliances. Three initiatives contributed to a more integrated focus on ECE early in our efforts to address the birth to grade 3 teaching continuum. These involved:

- Creating the ECE field endorsement addressing requirements for the Nebraska Inclusive Early Childhood Education (Birth to Grade 3) Teaching Certificate. This was co-developed by faculty in three departments—Child, Youth and Families; Elementary Education; and Special Education; and involved courses and practica across all three units. It was the first such certification in Nebraska.
- Creating the Kit and Dick Schmoker Reading Center, which supports K–12 students' proficiency in literacy skills. The center embraces a wide range of teaching strategies and involves students in all three ECE-related departments as reading instructors. The directorship of the center has rotated among faculty from the three departments since its inception and supports communication and shared teaching strategies within and across majors/programs.
- Creating the Nebraska Center for Research on Children, Youth, Families and Schools to conduct, support and share research with schools, community programs, practitioners, and policymakers. The center addresses issues such as school readiness, family-school partnerships, teacher coaching, and evaluation methodologies.

These initiatives were fundamental to enhancing "identity formation" around ECE throughout the college in teaching, research, and outreach.

AMOS: These are powerful examples of what's possible when smart people are willing to work together for meaningful change. Bringing together diverse perspectives provides a platform for addressing many of the issues we have raised throughout our discussion. As I consider what ECE curriculum and teaching/pedagogy should look like in the future, I agree that what future teachers experience in their higher-ed preparation is critical to moving our field forward. I especially like the move to a Birth to Grade 3 teaching certification and the emphasis on a wide range of teaching strategies. The certification issue is complex because individual states control teacher licensure, but as a field we can do all we can to move in that direction. Broadening our approach to ECE teaching/pedagogy will be challenging for other reasons.

As I was preparing to retire, I was invited to contribute a chapter to *The Handbook of Early Childhood Teacher Education* [2015]. My task was to propose alternative perspectives on pedagogy, and my response in that chapter spelled out some specific ways to broaden how ECE teachers are prepared to deliver instruction. I proposed a continuum of teaching approaches that purposefully pushed the limits on both ends. Here's the list: direct instruction; scaffolding; teaching for thinking; multiple literacies pedagogy; culturally responsive teaching; critical pedagogy (including critical literacy approaches); and postmodern approaches (as influenced by queer theory, deconstruction, postcolonial theory, poststructuralism, and feminist poststructuralism). I can see today that many of these approaches (the last ones for sure) would be cannon fodder for the right-wing extremists who are trying to control what gets taught and how it gets taught across the education spectrum. But the point is still good: Our children are growing up in a postmodern world, and it's our job as ECE professionals to utilize all the knowledge, expertise, and insight we can muster to provide programs that enhance the lives of all young children.

In terms of ECE curriculum in the future, I think we can introduce more genuine subject-matter content than has traditionally been included in pre-K programs. I am firmly opposed to pushing standards-driven models down into preschools. These regimes have had a terrible impact on K–3 education and beyond. But I can foresee a future where teachers work from curriculum materials that include subject-matter elements that should be intentionally taught, as opposed to assuming that young children will spontaneously construct the knowledge and build the skills they need by participating in engaging exploratory activities.

MARJORIE: Throughout this chapter we've noted ECE's need for expanded pedagogical strategies and approaches. Those you propose above fit that need well. I concur that accurate factual knowledge has an important place in ECE classrooms, as do a variety of teaching methods. Not surprisingly, that instruction can be viewed along a continuum ranging from exploratory play and guided discovery to problem-solving and direct instruction. The overarching ECE purpose we have been discussing throughout these pages represents a lofty goal that ECE will pursue for years to come. Thus, ECE remains a work in progress. Refer to Figure 5.1 for a visual depiction of where we have been and where I hope we will proceed relative to ECE pedagogy and curricula.

Figure 5.1. Demonstrated Sequence for Achieving Stronger Mission Identity in ECE

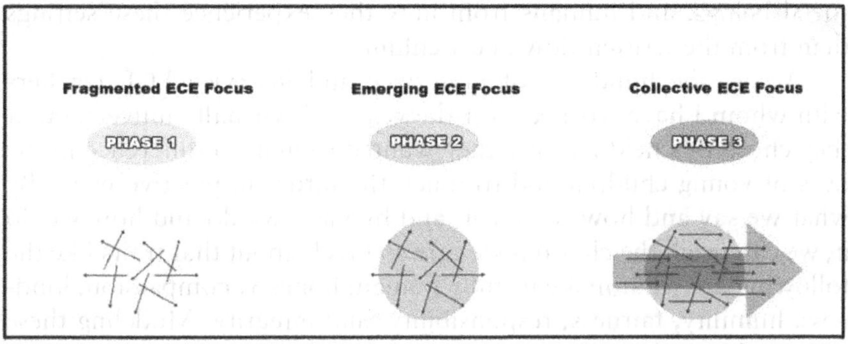

In Phase 1, various members of the ECE community had their own interpretations about what constituted the common ECE mission and what it looked like in action. Amos, our early days as students and beginning teachers were examples of this orientation. Many ideas were floated, tested, accepted, or rejected. We were all feeling our way and figuring out basics.

During Phase 2, the field began to coalesce around a central philosophy that defined who would be served, who would work with children, and what should go on in ECE classrooms. We have spent decades identifying, debating, and evaluating those details. These activities contribute to an Emerging ECE Focus, with some related initiatives but many independent strands too.

Phase 3 marks a time of increasing coalescence around central ideas across audiences and programs. Mission, philosophy, strategies, resources, and accountability may be similar or shared. Still, some independent activities and outcomes remain, allowing for individuation as needed.

This model is applicable to the entire field as well as specific programs. I would ask our readers, where do you see your ECE program in this diagram? If it is not in Phase 2 or 3, what would it take to move forward? That is where the future lies. That is the future you can help shape.

AMOS: As I think about curriculum and teaching at any level, I am reminded that in all educational settings powerful lessons are being internalized because of the ways classrooms are set up, expectations are communicated, and values are enacted. Every teaching/learning context includes what has been called a "hidden curriculum."

Lessons are "hidden" because they are unexamined, but they don't have to be. Young children learn more about themselves as learners, social beings, and humans from how they experience these settings than from the written-down curriculum.

Across the hundreds of preservice and inservice ECE teachers with whom I have worked over the years, it's virtually universal that they chose this field because they wanted to make a difference in the lives of young children and to touch the future in positive ways. By what we say and how we say it, and by what we do and how we do it, we can teach the children we care so much about that traits like the following are what make us fully human: honesty, compassion, kindness, humility, fairness, responsibility, and integrity. Modeling these traits in big and small ways gives ECE professionals a way to touch the future by being the change we want to see. The world has never needed it more.

Reflections on the Curriculum and Pedagogy in Early Childhood Education Conversation

Andrew J. Stremmel

What should young children be learning? How should teachers help them learn it? These questions, in the most practical sense, define curriculum and pedagogy. Curriculum, on one level, is everything that goes on in the life of the classroom or school—the unanticipated and unintended as well as the planned, the hidden as well as the overt, the experienced as well as the stated. Pedagogy is the excellence of teaching, a relationship of practical action between adults and children. More than just teaching strategies, pedagogy involves knowing how to act in a specific situation; knowing each child individually; knowing how children develop and learn; and understanding that the relationships teachers establish with children are always the best guide to determining what and how to teach.

The perspectives shared in this chapter reflect those of two well-established and innovative scholars who began their careers wanting to be teachers, albeit via differing pathways. Amos Hatch taught in an early elementary program that followed applied behavioral analysis, and Marjorie Kostelnik's teaching focused on social-emotional learning. Both were involved in leadership positions in NAEYC, and Marjorie became dean of a large Midwestern university. Though each presents a slightly different lens, both agree that the field remains divided in many ways and that this fragmentation impedes efforts to address the needs of children and teachers in all ECE classrooms, including recruiting new teachers to the profession and seeking public policy support for ECE.

The 1970s were all about finding the best curriculum approach, especially for children who were considered "culturally or linguistically" disadvantaged. However, curriculum effectiveness studies largely suggested that differing curricular approaches were not that important to child outcomes. Alternatively, for example, it may have been the teacher who made any difference in terms of how they implemented a particular curriculum. Much of the early research had flaws that related to the inadequacy of our theories and methods to inform curriculum practice and complexity of evaluating highly contextualized learning processes and environments involving children. Yet, as Marjorie points out, much of this research brought to the forefront the importance of research-based practices, program integrity, and ways of identifying high-quality teaching practices the field could embrace regardless of theoretical model (see Powell, 1987).

Tensions remain around what constitutes effective teaching practices and the mismatch between the reality of today's schools and traditional teacher preparation paradigms. Differences are further illustrated in current thinking about the role development plays in the design of curriculum and pedagogy. Developmental theory has had the most pervasive influence on curriculum, yet Amos has suggested that until recently the field has placed too much emphasis on development and not enough on learning. He argues that early childhood educators should intentionally include content in early childhood curricula and focus more on teaching for learning and less on facilitating development. For example, while children should be allowed to explore and manipulate an assortment of objects, systematic teaching of concepts and processes like classification, hypothesizing, investigation, interpretation, and communication are possible, along with real content. These "functional divergencies" (see Dewey, 1902) around teacher/subject-driven versus child–centered approaches, development versus learning, and the dissonance between what early childhood students learn in their coursework and what they do in their classrooms illustrate the ongoing struggles to define "good teaching."

Additional questions around curriculum and pedagogy focus on questions like, "Do we have sufficient focus on context and diversity, framing a particular discourse on what is normal or typical?" "Do children's capacities, education contexts, and societal expectations change across what we consider 'early childhood'?" And "How do we allow for more individual variation, given that there is no single best and efficient theory of learning and development?" Finally, early childhood educators must also be aware that they themselves—and their programs as a whole—bring their own experiences and contexts, in both the narrower and broader definitions, to their decision-making.

This is particularly important to consider when educators do not share the cultural contexts of the children they serve.

If the ultimate aim of education is to enhance the lives of all children, as both authors indicate, how do we design curriculum and teaching practices to meet the needs of all children? To adequately address what teaching and curriculum can be requires that we take a long, hard look at what counts in education. Is education about the dispensation of facts and information, or the creation of meaning and a transformed way of being, where every child is viewed as a whole and multidimensional human being? If our purpose is to help every child reach the full measure of their humanity, then teaching can never be reduced to technique, and curriculum can never be a one-size-fits-all approach. Learning, likewise, is not simply about comprehending the content of ideas; it is about discovering who one is in relation to new ideas and the questions they provoke. What is taught should be linked to how one lives and to the "real" questions of the children we teach. That is, what should matter is how education relates to human life and what is worth knowing.

Finally, to minimize the disconnect between what early childhood students learn in their teacher education programs and what they experience in schools, we can help them in three ways. We can help them to develop the knowledge, skills, and dispositions needed to teach a more diverse student population (including students from cultural and linguistically diverse backgrounds as well those with disabilities). We can better facilitate an enhanced understanding of an integrated curriculum model for instruction. Lastly, we can promote the use of inquiry to help them become the source and creator of the theoretical basis of their own teaching techniques and carry a positive attitude about lifelong learning into their professional lives. Achieving this outcome requires that prospective teachers, career teachers, and teacher educators have subject-matter expertise, as well as the ability to adapt curriculum and instruction to address individual learning characteristics.

Moreover, to more adequately prepare new teachers to respond to the changing needs of today's schools, the authors emphasize the need for a more collaborative approach among the disciplines that address ECE in our institutions to prepare all teachers to meet the leaning needs of all children. This will require, for example, programs that prepare special and general educators to work together and be accountable for the improved performance of all children. A powerful student-centered curriculum for learning to teach must be oriented around intellectual and practical tasks of teaching and the contexts of teachers' work. Teacher educators will need to adopt, encourage, and support central tasks of learning to teach related not only to subject-matter knowledge, but also inquiry, and identity and repertoire development (Feiman-Nemser, 2012).

QUESTIONS FOR DISCUSSION

1. The authors discuss the disconnect between what our field advocates as "appropriate" and what actually happens in schools with children ages 5–8. Do you think curriculum and pedagogy designed for pre-K children ought to look different than what is designed for school-age children? Are there developmental and learning differences across the birth-to-age-8 span to warrant such a consideration?
2. Amos mentions the overemphasis in early childhood education on young children's development and claims that learning provides the framework upon which early childhood classroom practices ought to be built. What are your thoughts about the learning versus development debate in thinking about curriculum and pedagogy?
3. What might a school look like that was designed to meet the needs of all children? What curriculum approach would you use? What would you be doing and what would the children be doing in the classroom?

FOR FURTHER READING

Couse, L. J., & Recchia, S. L. (2015). *Handbook of early childhood teacher education*. Routledge.

Dewey, J. (1902). *The child and the curriculum*. University of Chicago Press

Feiman-Nemser, S. (2012). *Teachers as learners*. Harvard Education Press.

Hatch, J. A. (2012). From theory to curriculum: Developmental theory and its relationship to curriculum and instruction in early childhood education. In N. File, J. J. Mueller, & D. B. Wisneski (Eds.), *Curriculum in early childhood education: Re-examined, rediscovered, renewed* (pp. 42–53). Routledge.

Kostelnik, M. J., Soderman, A. K., & Rupiper, M. (2024). *Developmentally appropriate curriculum: Effective practices in early childhood education* (8th ed.). Pearson Publishing.

Lash, M. (2019). Perspectives on early childhood curricula. In C. P. Brown, M. B. McMullen, & N. File (Eds.), *Wiley handbook of early childhood care and education* (pp. 261–277). Wiley Blackwell.

Mueller, J. J., & File, N. (Eds.). (2020). *Curriculum in early childhood education: Re-examined, reclaimed, renewed (*2nd ed.). Routledge.

Powell, D. R. (1987). Comparing preschool curricula and practices: The state of the research. In S. L. Kagan & E. F. Zigler (Eds.), *Early schooling: The national debate* (pp. 190–2011). Yale University Press.

CHAPTER 6

The Place of Infants and Toddlers in Early Childhood Education

Mary Benson McMullen and Susan L. Recchia

Mary Benson McMullen has been a professor of early childhood education at Indiana University since 1993. She received a B.S. from Michigan State University and M.S. and Ph.D. degrees in child development from Florida State University. She was an infant-toddler and preschool teacher, then program director, before joining IU. She teaches courses to preservice and inservice early childhood professionals, as well as doctoral students who will be ECE teacher educators. Mary's research involves quality early care and education for infants and toddlers; the healthy overall growth, development, learning, and well-being of children from birth to age 5; teaching beliefs and practices across cultures and contexts; and factors that ensure the well-being of ECE professionals. She is the author of numerous publications, including *On Being and Well-Being in Infant/Toddler Care and Education: Life Stories from Baby Rooms,* and the co-author of NAEYC's 2022 book, *Infants & Toddlers at Play: Choosing the Right Stuff for Learning & Development* with Dylan Brody.

Susan L. Recchia is Professor Emeritus at Teachers College, Columbia University, where she served as coordinator of the Early Childhood/Special Education Program and was faculty director of the Rita Gold Early Childhood Center. Her experience in infant child care and early intervention inspired her ways of preparing new teachers for inclusive early care and education for infants, children, and families. She engaged doctoral students in finding agency as early childhood teacher educators and researchers through multiple collaborations, preparing them for careers as leaders in the field. She was a New York 0–3 Network board member for 25 years and served two terms as co-president. She recently received a Distinguished Career

Contribution Award (AERA Critical Perspectives in ECE, 2023). She has authored, co-authored, and co-edited numerous articles, chapters, and books, including *Relationship-Based Care for Infants and Toddlers: Fostering Early Learning and Development Through Responsive Practice.*

WHEN YOU FIRST BEGAN YOUR CAREER, WHAT PLACE DID INFANTS AND TODDLERS AND THEIR CARE HAVE IN THE FIELD?

SUSAN: As an undergraduate in the early 1970s, I was delighted to secure an assistant teacher position working with young toddlers at the UCLA Child Care Center. At that time, this was one of two programs providing center-based child care for infants in Los Angeles. I was assigned to the toddler room, for children from 18 months to 2 1/2 years. I learned from two wonderful mentor teachers how to be present with infants and toddlers, follow their lead in play, and respond to their special ways of communicating. There was no set curriculum or standards. We spent our days observing the children, sharing our insights, responding to their initiations, and engaging in playful interactions and responsive caregiving. I had no idea at the time that the work we were engaged in was what we now embrace decades later as quality care for infants and toddlers.

When I graduated with my B.A., I hoped to work in a similar kind of center, but there were still very few center-based programs serving infants and toddlers. Most ECE centers required that children be potty-trained. The pay for caregivers was so low that I could not live on it; none of the programs I applied to offered health care, sick leave, or paid vacation days, not to mention any kind of a retirement plan! I took a job in an office to get by until my life took a turn that allowed me to find my dream job in a parent-infant cooperative offering care for infants and toddlers. I was hired to pay special attention to the youngest babies.

MARY: You were fortunate, Susan, to have had strong mentoring and exposure to positive infant-toddler practices early in your career. In the mid-1980s, when I first sought child care for my sons, ages 1 and 3, I chose a program because it was inexpensive and close to our home. I felt like I'd found a bargain! But my oldest son was unhappy and resisted being dropped off, and he was sullen and sometimes angry when I picked them up. As I progressed in my Child Development master's program, I soon became more critical of what we were experiencing. I felt it was a safe place, but the environment was loud and chaotic, and the staff seemed chronically disengaged.

Soon our family moved to a new home in Tallahassee; the boys began attending a NAEYC-accredited program nearby. What a change! Both boys were eager to "go to school" in the morning. We were always greeted warmly, and at pickup time, my boys were covered in sand, mud, or paint, and full of happy chatter about the day. I trusted the teachers the moment I met them and, over time, formed strong bonds with them and many other parents.

Soon after my third son was born, we moved to Indiana, and I became an infant caregiver. I loved this work. A few years later, I became director of the program—which I did not love. It was my first experience with the harsh realities and difficult choices that come with building yearly budgets, choices I now frame as moral and ethical. Could we continue to subsidize low parent fees with low teacher wages? Was it fair to charge so much more for infant-toddler care than for preschoolers? Where would children go if the family could no longer afford us?

SUSAN: I so loved working with the youngest infants. It was wonderful to have the time, space, and support to provide this kind of care. I didn't realize at the time how special it was. I worked 6 hours a day and did my M.A. at night. But soon the director informed me that she was leaving, and she wanted me to take over. Flattered with her confidence in me, I agreed.

Our center was created by a savvy group of university parents who formed a child care co-op with the help of a new grant from the state supporting low-income families. They turned a small house into a homey space for 13 babies, complete with a yard for outdoor play. To help lower the costs, parents contributed time each week caring for the children or helping with custodial tasks. It was an ideal setup to build community between the staff and the families.

As director, I was responsible for coordinating schedules, managing the budget, overseeing the teaching staff, making sure regulations were being followed, and running parent and staff meetings. I also worked with the children for a good part of my day, and if a teacher was sick, I usually had to take her shift. I found myself working 12-hour days just to keep up.

As a young, inexperienced director, not yet a parent myself, I really struggled when issues arose with parents. When I became aware that some of them were hiding parts of their income to qualify for the grant subsidy, I was so disheartened. As much as I believed in helping families have access to quality child care, I couldn't condone this form of cheating the system. Eventually, the combination of overload, burnout, and a need to write my master's thesis drove me to resign.

MARY: I too *loved* my years working with infants. But as you know, not everyone respects this work. My own colleagues used to say, for example, "When are you going to graduate from the baby room and be a real teacher?" "You're so good, what a waste to keep you working with infants!" I was irritated by some who patronizingly called me a "saint," and those who called me a "babysitter." Such responses made me feel hurt and angry, and on reflection, I realize they were simultaneously dismissive of me and disrespectful of very young children.

Things weren't much better in the 1990s when, as a new assistant professor, I applied for my first research grant. The feedback I got on my first grant proposal was: "What on earth could you learn 'hanging out' with a bunch of babies." I momentarily questioned my career choice, but rather than give up, I decided it was up to me to help others understand *why* it is important to learn about these first years. I became passionate about learning all I could to improve infant-toddler care and education for children, professionals, and families.

Within a few years, interest in birth to-age 3 became increasingly relevant. Everyone seemed to become fascinated with what neuroscientists were finding about the importance of the infant-toddler period. Books like *Rethinking the Brain* in 1997 and *From Neurons to Neighborhoods* in 2000 touted what we in early childhood had known for decades, that infants and toddlers are amazingly capable and that positive, trusting relationships and early experiences matter!

SUSAN: In the late 1970s, most people didn't think of infant-toddler child care as education. The idea that our work with infants could be more than a service for working parents hadn't really registered. There was no teacher certification below kindergarten, and qualifications for working with under-5s varied from place to place. There were very few rules about how to work with infants. We were inventing infant-toddler curriculum in the process, drawing mostly from what we knew about child development and simply being with babies.

In my M.A. program I studied with Rose Bromwich, the first professor at the college to introduce courses on working with infants. She wrote and taught about her work with families with infants and toddlers with disabilities at a time when ideas about early intervention were still emerging. Inspired by her work, I changed the course of my studies, and found a part-time job working in a therapeutic nursery school serving preschoolers with visual impairments. The director hired me even though I had no formal training in special education. She said there were many experts there who I would learn from, but what I had was more important to her—a way of interacting with young children that was authentic and caring. This is what the babies had taught me.

Several years later, I became their infant-toddler specialist, providing support for parents and children individually and in groups. Although I was often asked, "How do you teach a baby? What do they actually learn?," in some ways, early intervention added a certain legitimacy to teaching 0–3. There was still no specialization in working with this age group, but programs were beginning to be developed in response to parent advocacy.

MARY: I've learned through my career how much *words matter*. I like the term "infant-toddler specialist" you used. Although still mostly associated with early intervention, the term could apply more broadly. So many words in our field inadequately describe infant-toddler work, especially academic terms like "teaching," "curriculum," and "classrooms." Regardless, it seems that most who work in infant-toddler childcare prefer the title "teacher," because, they have told me, it helps for they themselves and for others to see them as professionals. I understand this desire and agree that what we call ourselves and how we talk about what we do *is* important. But academic terms leave out an important ingredient that defines us: care. I try to promote "care" and "caring" as central to infant-toddler work, but such terms are also challenging. In a field dominated by a belief in the importance of relationships, a term such as "care*giver*," for instance, sends a discordant message.

Some professionals, especially proponents of the Resources for Infant Educarers (RIE) Approach, call themselves "educarers," but I've always found this term somewhat clumsy. Certainly, care and learning in the first 3 years are inseparable. But do we have to *teach* for the child to *learn*? In an article I wrote in 2010, "Confronting the Baby Blues," I bemoaned time spent in a behaviorist infant room. The staff there claimed credit for *teaching* the young infants to achieve typical developmental milestones, like rolling over and pulling up to cruise along the furniture.

I end where I started: Words matter.

SUSAN: Words do matter, and what we call ourselves and our work can change how caring for infants and toddlers is perceived in the field and the world. I never struggled with calling myself an infant caregiver, as care is so intrinsic to being with babies. Yet many of my students also prefer to be called teachers, as if they weren't "teachers," infants and toddlers couldn't be learning! How do we fully capture the essence of quality infant care and education in any label? What I once just did intuitively so many years ago I now understand as deeply complex and nuanced.

HOW HAVE CHANGES IN SOCIETY AND IN THE ATTENTION PAID TO INFANTS AND TODDLERS IN RESEARCH OVER TIME IMPACTED CHILD CARE FOR VERY YOUNG CHILDREN?

MARY: My first awareness of how society viewed infants and toddlers occurred when I encountered the child care "good" versus "bad" debates of the 1980s. It was soon after my second son was born in 1985 when I started graduate school. I joined the ranks of millions of women juggling home and school/work responsibilities, learning quickly how hard this was with a breastfed infant and a busy 2-year-old. I was young and idealistic, believing the "women can have it all" notion prevalent at that time.

I struggled with the logistics of finding someone my husband and I trusted to be with our children and questioned how we could afford it. But worst of all, I suffered from "mommy guilt." From popular books and magazine articles I read at the time, I knew I wasn't alone. I discovered that many others were haunted by doubts and questions like mine: Was I being selfish going back to school? How could I leave these precious children in the arms of someone else? Would my very young children be "okay" without me?

Around this time, the issue of "who's minding our children" had exploded into a hot political and societal debate. Everyone had an opinion about how best to care for babies and young children. "Women belong at home with their kids," some shouted; "Women who put their careers on hold will suffer," others retorted; "Child care is bad for kids!" claimed some of the loudest voices. The so-called "mommy wars" were primarily fueled by politicians, policymakers, opinion writers, and conflicting research findings. Women were pitted against one another, in sharp contrast to the decades before when they united to fight for equal rights. At this time, women who wanted to stay home with their children felt attacked, as did those of us who needed or chose child care. We needed to find more and better ways to support each other's choices.

SUSAN: I began my doctoral studies when my second child was 16 months old in 1987. I was the only mother in my doctoral cohort. Bowlby's attachment theory was all the rage! The implied understanding, that insecure attachments between infants and mothers would likely result in later social challenges, affecting relationships across the life span, did give me pause as I negotiated child care for my son.

I took a course in Social Development with Carolee Howes, one of the few researchers who was studying child care using the Waters Attachment Q-Sort to look at teacher-child relationships. She found that secure relationships do happen with child care teachers under the right conditions, and they do not detract from children's attachments with their mothers. But, not surprisingly, caregiver-child attachments look different for mothers and teachers.

Later, some researchers began to question this one-size-fits-all way of thinking about attachment and whether the measures made sense within different environmental, familial, and cultural contexts. The question is no longer such a simple binary of whether child care is good or bad for babies, but has taken on greater complexity as we consider children's and families' rights to high-quality early care.

MARY: Yes, thankfully we've moved beyond the simple binaries of "good versus bad" and "appropriate versus inappropriate." I reminisced about such changes when I read the most recent fourth edition of NAEYC's *Developmentally Appropriate Practice* (DAP). I began my career around the time the first edition was published in 1987, and I'm nearing retirement with its fourth release. How far we've come as a field—and I've come personally—in the ongoing journey to understand how best to interact with infants, toddlers, young children, and their families! And one of the biggest areas of growth in the field and society is greater recognition of the importance of supporting development, learning, and well-being during the first 3 years.

It was the first DAP book in my early days of graduate school that led me to question the adequacy of that first child care program my children attended, mentioned earlier. The book opened my eyes, allowing me to see how the theories of Piaget, Erikson, and Bowlby and Ainsworth could be applied to real life with real children in group settings. Along with work by Carolee Howes, whom you mention, and others, I found ways to speak back to those who were convinced by scholars such as Jay Belsky that child care would do irreparable harm to children [see reflective essay]. Most people had no choice! Increasingly, child care was becoming a necessity, even for infants. It was then that I became committed to learning all I could to do something to improve child care for children and families. In 1991 [*Journal of Home Economics*], I wrote in favor of national family leave, saying: "Current economic conditions make it necessary for most [parents] to be employed, not so they can attain luxuries, but so they can meet family expenditures."

SUSAN: Although we've increased government support for pre-K programs, we have not come to terms with the need for quality infant-toddler child care. Regulations and licensing requirements vary from state to state and focus more on health and safety issues than responsive care and early education. Most families must bear the weight of finding and financing care on their own.

Despite what research has told us for decades about the significance of the first 3 years of life as foundational to later learning and healthy development, sadly, far too many babies have been and continue to be cared for in settings that are providing mediocre care, at best. Howes, Phillips, and Whitebook reported this in 1992, yet little had changed by the time Lally published *For Our Babies: Ending the Invisible Neglect of America's Infants* in 2013.

Research has also documented the need for better-prepared teachers to provide high-quality child care for infants and toddlers, yet early childhood degree programs in the United States tend to give inadequate attention to these critical early years in preparing early childhood teachers for work in the field as reported by Horm, Hyson, and Winton in 2013. New technologies have provided amazing insights into the infant brain, clearly demonstrating the impact of early responsive caregiving on infants' overall well-being, yet there remains a large gap between what we know from brain science and what actually happens in many infant-toddler child care centers.

MARY: You're so right. Despite the brain research, infant-toddler care and education and the professional preparation of its staff remain underresearched, and too little of what is learned translates into practice. There are many possible reasons for this, such as the inadequate specialized preparation of birth-to-3 professionals that you note. But also, there is a lack of understanding by preschool administrators about this age group, and perhaps more disheartening, it's because work with our youngest children remains undervalued in our society.

The Howes, Phillips, and Whitebook 1992 study should have served as a wake-up call to all Americans. At the time it was published,

I was distraught to learn that on average preschool children were in "mediocre" settings (as sad as that is!), but even more alarmed to learn that on average, infant-toddler child care was of "poor quality." "Poor" meant that babies' health and safety were at risk. Although we have no data for direct comparison to that earlier study, I have to believe we have improved since 1992, in part because of wider awareness of issues of quality and the implementation of quality rating systems (QRS) by most states. But we still have much to do to improve the quality of the day-to-day experiences of children, families, and professionals in infant-toddler child care.

Speaking of quality, I return to our discussion of how words matter. Through much of my career I have collaborated with early childhood scholars across the world. It has made me sensitive to how notions of "best practice" and "high-quality" are understood in different cultures, countries, and contexts. What diverse groups of people believe about how to raise children, the goals of families and societies, and how they impact definitions of quality in infant-toddler care and education are areas of our field that are fascinating, complex, and very important to consider.

SUSAN: Thankfully, more research is focusing on the power of cultural contexts in determining what works best for infants, toddlers, and families. These findings are critical to child care practice, particularly as the U.S. population becomes more diverse. Using descriptors like "responsive caregiving" might seem unclear to those outside the field, but umbrella terms like this allow room for interpretation within differing cultural contexts.

How families become attuned to their babies is at the heart of responsive caregiving, but their actual ways of behaving may look very different. Cultural differences between caregivers and the children and families they serve must also be considered, particularly in infant-toddler care, where caregivers are more diverse than other groups of teachers. Studies have demonstrated that caring is deeply connected to our own early experiences and what we have learned about caring for babies within our own cultures.

Intimate tasks like feeding, diapering, sleeping, and comforting require more than following a set of guidelines for what children "should" be able to do at a given age. Learning to read and understand their cues involves a deeper knowledge about infants' lives within their families, where a baby's expectations of being cared for emerge. Although we have made progress in identifying descriptors for responsive caregiving, it's important not to lose sight of the need for caregivers' knowledge of both their own cultural inclinations and those of the children and families they care for.

MARY: Our increasing awareness of the importance of differences in beliefs and values associated with raising children and the embracing and celebrating of diversity have resulted in some of the most impactful changes to our notions of quality infant-toddler care and education since the 1980s. These changes have compelled us to seek better ways to connect and build trusting relationships with families in infant-toddler settings, ways that respect and support their home cultures, languages, and belief systems. While we have embraced relationship-based and holistic principles of practice for quite some time (e.g., individualized care, being "in tune" and sensitively responsive, attending to the needs of the whole child), our understanding of these ideas as professionals and scholars has deepened. We now promote the idea that respect for infants and toddlers as individual persons requires us to come to know them and their families well, to understand who they are now in the moment while preparing them for who they will become, and to support their sense of belonging within their families, cultures, and communities. Changes in society have led us to this better place in which the recognition of and respect for difference is now a hallmark of quality in infant-toddler care and education.

HOW HAVE SHIFTS OVER TIME WITHIN THE FIELD IMPACTED WHAT ACTUALLY OCCURS IN INFANT-TODDLER SETTINGS? HAS THIS MOVED THE FIELD FORWARD OR NOT?

MARY: Despite our acknowledgment of a research-practice gap, slow but steady changes across my 40 years in the profession have moved us forward as a field. Notably, more attention is now paid to the first 3 years by scholars, practitioners, teacher educators, and policymakers, resulting in improved child care quality for infants, toddlers, families, and professionals.

For example, there has been significant advancement in supporting relationship-based practices since we started our careers. This is a result, in part, of our evolving understanding of attachment theory, discussed earlier. More recently, newer generations of psychoanalytic, developmental, and early learning theorists have expanded upon Erikson's psychosocial theories of trust and further supported the lifelong impact of social-emotional learning and development during the first 3 years. Such scholarship supports practices such as continuity of care and primary care models, and further, it enhances arguments for the critical importance of infant-toddler social-emotional learning, development, and well-being.

Other important ideas come from critical theorists who have advanced our understanding of diversity and the benefits of culturally responsive infant-toddler practices. Interpretations of Vygotsky's sociocultural theory have helped us understand that all learning is socially mediated. And child rights advocates and the United Nations Convention on the Rights of the Child have moved us forward in thinking about the need to support children's autonomy and agency, overall physical and emotional health and well-being, and their right to play. But while these and other areas of learning and progress should be celebrated, we must keep in mind those infants, toddlers, and families who are left out or who have not yet benefited from these advancements in knowledge and practice. All discussions about progress must acknowledge the absence of equitable access to affordable, high-quality infant-toddler care and education.

SUSAN: Yes, in our eagerness to see change happen faster, it is easy to overlook just how much we have learned about infants and toddlers that can be applied to our work. Infant-toddler scholars understand what it takes to provide high-quality infant-toddler care, and we have gotten much better at articulating the kinds of environments, caregiver qualities, and administrative supports that are needed to make it happen. Unfortunately, however, as a country we do not really have an infrastructure in place to provide this kind of care across communities. High-quality care too often comes with a big price tag.

The number of infant-toddler child care centers across the country has grown exponentially since I started in the field. Over time, these centers have become increasingly regulated by licensing agencies. Although it is important to make sure health and safety regulations are in place, and to monitor programs to see that they are meeting the established criteria for things like group size, child vaccinations, cleanliness, food safety practices, caregiver qualifications, and child-to-caregiver ratios, many of the other criteria that we have come to associate with quality care are not being assessed.

Furthermore, some of the licensing requirements seem to undermine aspects of quality like continuity of care and responsive individualized caregiving. For example, when concerns about children's safety require that infants must move to a new group once they begin to crawl or walk, not only are opportunities for mixed-age groups restricted, but often continuity of care becomes disrupted. When concerns about never having infants out of a caregiver's sight require that they all sleep in the main playroom or at the same time, individual sleep needs cannot be adequately addressed.

In my work supervising students in a variety of practicum placements, I have seen state regulations interpreted in ways that I believe compromise infant-toddler care and create added stress for children, caregivers, and administrators alike. Centers face many challenges as they try to balance expectations for compliance with meeting individual needs.

MARY: So many of these rules and regulations designed to "protect" children work against full implementation of many of the advancements to the field that we have discussed. But also, they inhibit free and unrestricted movement and healthy risk-taking in infants and toddlers. Further, they often undermine the spontaneity, natural responsiveness, and availability of the infant-toddler care and education staff.

Certainly, neither of us would seek to ban regulations and procedures that keep everyone healthy and safe. We have learned much in our careers about things like nutrition, toxic plastics, using sunscreen, childproofing, and so on. But when regulations replace the decision-making of well-educated infant-toddler specialists and their ability to be responsive to children's and families' needs, they have gone too far. When rules require completion of so many checklists, paperwork, and reports that they limit time spent with children, something is wrong. When standards enforce practices counter to what we know supports the development, learning, and well-being of children, things must change.

Where I live, state licensing requires continuity of care and the assignment of primary caregivers. The way this is implemented, however, varies greatly, with many programs violating the good intentions of the policy. But I can say that slowly and steadily, a growing number of infant-toddler settings throughout the state are implementing stronger relationship-based practices that serve as models for others. This tends, however, to be in higher-cost programs, bringing me back to our mutual concern about the cost of quality infant-toddler child care.

SUSAN: I guess the good news is that we are changing our thinking as a field not only about the necessity of quality infant-toddler child care, but also about its significance in the lives of children, families, and communities. More recent scientific findings on 0–3 have given new credibility to what those of us in the field have known intuitively for decades: Infants and toddlers are active agents in their own learning, and early experiences within relationship-based care have an incredible influence on future growth and development. It is encouraging to know that in your state, Mary, some of this knowledge has been written into the licensing regulations, but as you say, how the constructs are interpreted in practice can vary from program to program.

I have also been encouraged to see more emphasis on play-based learning in some areas of early intervention, although I believe there is much more work to be done in that arena. As more wonderful ideas circulate about respecting babies, placing children and families at the center of early care and education, and guaranteeing children's rights to play, learning, and belonging, it is inevitable that they will find their way into practice, at least in some places. The challenge of being able to bring them to scale across the field remains a steep hill to climb.

So, in thinking about whether we are moving forward, I guess I would say yes, but in fits and starts! We have some amazing centers that are already engaging in many of these exemplary practices. Yet in other centers, which may be closer to the norm, they cannot be fully supported. Staff turnover is rampant in child care settings, in part due to inadequate salaries and benefits, but also due to the stress created by inadequate or unreliable support for the challenging work infant-toddler teachers must do to provide quality care.

MARY: You bring up an interesting point about more generalized infant-toddler care and education's influence on the emphasis on play in early intervention. I have seen the influence between the two fields flow back and forth over our careers, with each field learning and growing in mutually supportive ways.

One thing from early intervention that has influenced me and has changed how I prepare future infant-toddler professionals is the notion of family-centered practices. At the start of my career, it was more common for us to speak of "parents"; now, most of us have adopted the broader and more inclusive term "families." And while I have always promoted the importance of infant-toddler professionals working with parents/families, when I started teaching, I framed it as "keeping them informed," or "getting them more involved." This practice failed to fully acknowledge and respect the role of those most important adults in the lives of the infants or toddlers. This way of thinking implied that all decisions about the care and education of the infants and toddlers were to be made by the professionals and imposed upon the child/family.

We now stress that embracing family-centeredness compels infant-toddler professionals to build relationships of trust and mutual respect, to think of themselves as partners *with* the family, supporting *their* goals and values in mutually agreed-upon ways. This has been a significant advancement in our thinking, putting at the center the very people who understand best what it means for that child to be a part of their family, community, and culture.

SUSAN: I definitely think there is more shared learning between the fields of infant-toddler child care and early intervention. Many more children are receiving special education services within their community child care centers, which has allowed for cross-fertilization of ideas and practices. Although there are still challenges to working collaboratively, the benefits, when things go well, can make such a powerful impact on everyone involved. Child care teachers learn special skills and strategies from special educators that can enhance their connections with children, while special educators observe and learn from child care providers about working with children in a natural context. Children with disabilities and their families have access to the child care community, its resources, and experiences available to others.

Because many infants and toddlers with special needs enter child care before they are assessed or determined to need services, infant-toddler caregivers are positioned to be first responders as needs arise. Open collaborations bring greater awareness and reduce stigma around early intervention. Partnering with families to access services, caregivers become part of a supportive network focused on children's and families' well-being. For many infants and toddlers and their families, early intervention can have a life-changing impact on their future.

MARY: I loved how you spoke earlier, Susan, of how so many "wonderful ideas circulate." It brought an image to my mind of these ideas that advance the field as going round and round, like a snowball gathering substance as it rolls down a big hill. I can almost picture this small ball of ideas as it grows bigger and bigger, collecting loose threads of ideas and new theories along the way, always spinning in a forward direction. Let's hope that big ball of progress continues to pick up speed as it goes along.

WHAT SHIFTS DO YOU HOPE TO SEE IN THE FUTURE FOR INFANTS AND TODDLERS AND BIRTH TO THREE CARE AND EDUCATION?

SUSAN: There are reasons to be hopeful about the future of infant-toddler care and education. First, I do think that we are in a political and societal moment for truly reconsidering the critical importance of reliable, supportive, high-quality child care for working families. In the face of the COVID-19 pandemic, it became all too clear that families with young children cannot be full-fledged members of the workforce without it. In calling attention to the ongoing challenge of providing support for caregivers so they can provide support for children and families, this international crisis pushed us as a country to think more deeply about the ways that our current child care systems are falling short. Although the lack of adequate support for infant-toddler child care was not a secret before the pandemic, moments like these can create opportunities for transformation, and I hope that we will not lose our momentum in this one.

A wonderful first step would be to fully integrate infant-toddler care into early education, moving past the artificial boundaries that have been created over the years. We already have scientific evidence showing the significance of the first 3 years of life as the foundation for future learning and development; research has shown that at least 80% of the adult brain is developed by the time a child turns 3, and this development happens best in the context of reciprocal relationships and nurturing environments. We need to see high-quality child care and early education as not only a national responsibility, but as a right for children and families. We also need to find the political will to support increased funding for infant-toddler child care to ease the financial burden on parents.

MARY: I, too, have become more hopeful than ever recently about the future of infant-toddler care and education. You are correct that the need for more, and more equitable, high-quality child care staffed by fully qualified professionals was never a secret. But it was predominantly early childhood educators and scholars, along with families, who cried out for this, the concerns falling mostly on deaf ears. Now the call is somehow more urgent, more intense, and coming from politicians, economists, and business leaders, among many others. I hope that the newfound appreciation and valuing of child care that emerged from our shared global pandemic experience survives the immediate crisis.

I hope we can seize the moment and not let the opportunity pass us by. The early childhood workforce together with families must rally support within our communities from all sectors. We must move forward with advocacy, education, and strategic planning that will bring about the change we want. We must also vote for candidates who understand how to support and value infants, toddlers, young children, and their families.

I agree with you that it should be a national responsibility, and hope for a future in which it will be seen as such. By "national" I mean that everyone, including our governments and our other major institutions, as well as scholars and practitioners, must work toward a common goal of increasing the availability and affordability of high-quality care and education for all who need it. But I would add a note of caution here about considering a "nationalized" system, curriculum model, or one-size-fits all standards for our field. Thinking back to our conversation in Question 3 about rules, regulations, and how they all too often interfere with recommended practices gives me pause. I find myself thinking of the phrase "be careful what you wish for" when I consider some of the potential unintended consequences of a nationwide system.

SUSAN: I think this is one of the biggest dilemmas we are facing in the field of education at all levels today. In trying to create "standards" that are meant to "improve" quality, we move toward a kind of homogenization that undercuts all that we know about the need to be individually and culturally responsive, and to embed meaningful learning experiences within the context of diverse communities. When standards are rigidly constructed with a one-size-fits-all model, we lose the ability to honor individual rights and needs. Our spoken goals of "bridging the gap" or "widening the playing field" to create more opportunities can end up marginalizing, excluding, and even harming young learners.

In terms of infant-toddler care and education, as we have said before, environments must be safe and protective, but rules should be considered through a lens of what is good for children and families, with room for flexible decision-making when unexpected situations arise. Administrators and caregivers should be able to consider what is most equitable within a particular community. And what is equitable is not always "equal"; not everyone needs or desires the same things.

When I dream about the future of infant-toddler child care, I imagine environments that are less institutional and more homelike, ideally with mixed-aged groups of children, which are naturally designed to allow continuity of care, especially for the youngest infants. I see more intentional practices that welcome parents as partners in their children's care. I hope for changes in the ways that we honor the work of infant-toddler caregivers, not only with a living wage, but with the respect they deserve as educators.

MARY: It's been clear to me from the start of our conversation that we have similar values, beliefs, and even some experiences when it comes to infant-toddler care and education, past and present. And now, I see we share similar dreams for its future. Thus, in the tradition of actors doing improvisation, I begin my response to you by saying, "yes; and." *Yes*, I too hope for a future where our professionals are elevated to their deserved place among other educators and that they are provided a living wage and benefits. *And*, as a field and as a society, I hope in the future that we continue to identify, implement, and advocate for policies and practices that support the overall physical, psychological, and emotional health and well-being of infant-toddler professionals.

Wages, benefits, and professional identity are indeed critical components of the overall health and well-being of our workforce. But these things are just part of what infant-toddler professionals need and what motivates them to stay in their current positions and in the field. Turnover wreaks havoc on the kind of relationship-based care we both endorse as an element of quality in child care. It severs important relationships built on mutual and long-term knowledge and trust, disrupting continuity of care for the children and families. We also know that professionals who spend their days preoccupied and distracted by thoughts of being "anywhere but here" have diminished capacity to care, meaning they cannot focus on the children and families as fully and as sensitively as those who are satisfied or happy in their roles. Thus, turnover and the risk of turnover impact quality as we know it.

So I hope for a day where we do a better job helping infant-toddler professionals to experience a sense of belonging to the wider early childhood care and education community with others who respect them as colleagues. I want us to help them feel engaged and intellectually challenged at work, and that their accomplishments contribute in important ways. Also, I want them to experience senses of agency, power, and control over decision-making in their daily work lives.

SUSAN: We really have our work cut out for us! And it will require rallying the "whole village" to do justice to what we know we need.

I am encouraged by actions at a national level, like the Universal Child Care and Early Learning Act, recently introduced by Senator Warren and then-Representative (now Secretary of the Interior) Haaland. This legislation speaks to some of the issues we've been talking about regarding affordability and quality and acknowledges the significance of a well-prepared and equitably paid child care workforce. Has the moment finally arrived where the dream of having universal access to quality early care and education in the United States, as we see in some European countries, can become a reality?

As systems for early care and education continue to be expanded and refined, we will have to work very hard to hold onto the essence of quality responsive care, making sure that those elements that we have emphasized throughout this chapter are honored. I, too, am frightened by the possibility of imposing standards and regulations that undermine the spirit of quality care for infants and toddlers. I think about some of the changes that have come about in various universal pre-K and kindergarten programs within the United States, where academic readiness has dominated the curriculum and undermined developmental opportunities for young children to learn at their own pace.

Rather than designing programs with a top-down approach, where teaching and learning are conceptualized as meeting particular academic end goals, programs for infants and toddlers must start by meeting babies and families where they are, recognizing the unique ways that infants and their caregivers come to know the world together. Maintaining a high level of consciousness about creating spaces for agentic exploration, meaningful interactions with adults and peers, individualized and responsive caregiving, and support for staff and families will be critical to this vision.

MARY: Thank you, Susan. I really enjoyed engaging in this conversation with you, sharing our experiences, challenges and insights, and our dreams for ever-improving infant-toddler care and education.

SUSAN: And thank you, Mary. It's been great looking back and looking forward together on a topic that we both care so deeply about that has been integral to both our personal and professional lives.

Reflections on the Place of Infants and Toddlers Conversation

Nancy File

The place occupied by infants and toddlers in early childhood is unique. This is apparent in how Mary McMullen and Susan Recchia discuss issues such as what it is we do with infants and toddlers, what approaches are valued, and even what practitioners might call themselves. While a 4-year-old may be (wrongly) assumed to be a smaller version of a primary-grade child, it is clear that infants and toddlers are not just smaller versions of a preschooler. Thus, particular words have come to reflect values and ideology in this area of the field, including responsiveness, authenticity, and relationship-based practices. Susan found exemplars of these practices very early in her experience; Mary described the effort of finding good care for her own children. Both contributors acknowledge that the field still struggles with fully realizing high-quality experiences for the youngest children.

Infants and toddlers were not front and center earlier in our history. Originally the domain of university-sponsored intervention programs or a localized response to a need for care, the area has experienced exponential growth within the last few decades. According to data from the U.S. Bureau of Labor Statistics (obtained from bls.gov), in 1975, 47.4% of women with children under 18 participated in the workforce. At the same time, 34.3% of women with a child under 3 years of age were in the workforce. By 2020, the percentage of women in the workforce with children under 18 grew to 72.5%. The growth was proportionately higher for women with a child under 3, reaching 65.6% in 2020, close to the overall participation rate of women with minor children.

Still, in the United States there are insufficient care options for the children of these families. As discussed by both contributors, programs for infants and toddlers face high costs because fewer children are enrolled per caregiver. Often, salaries are lower for infant-toddler caregivers compared to those who work with older children. Both Mary and Susan relate these challenges to the need to develop new systems and supports within the field. Demonstrating the interrelatedness of the topics chosen for this volume, we encourage readers to think about infant-toddler care when reading the chapter on early childhood systems.

Susan and Mary introduced conflicts that began in the mid-1980s, gripped by the question: Is child care detrimental to babies? The question reflects both societal conflict over the place of women as well as a not-uncommon early phase of research, the question of whether something is good or harmful (a simple question also applied initially to other complex situations, such as child care for older children and the first efforts to place children with special needs in the "least restrictive environment"). As described by Mary, the question was met with a wide range of opinions from many fronts, a phenomenon that weighed heavily on women.

In this case, researcher Jay Belsky sparked the question in 1986 when he reviewed research and proposed that babies who experienced more hours in care were at greater risk of developing an insecure attachment with their mothers, which could then lead to later difficulties (published in *Zero to Three*). Reaction followed with a journal special edition (*Early Childhood Research Quarterly*, published in September 1988) examining various perspectives, including how research is conducted and the fact that Belsky's conclusion did not stem from following babies in child care through a significant portion of their childhood. A large study was launched across several locations nationwide, enrolling families very early on and following them for years. The findings suggested that the initial question was indeed overly simplistic. Child care experiences vary from frankly terrible to quite wonderful. Babies may experience stability or instability in their child care arrangements over time. Families also have an influence on their children. In the end, the common interpretation was that early child care is not in itself a risk, but that many factors interact to play a part in how children and families fare. New research methods were developed (Susan mentioned the Q-sort), which replaced an earlier method in which children were observed for their reaction when their mothers left them with a researcher and then returned to them in a lab setting (the Strange Situation). Young children in care experience daily good-byes and reunions with their family members, changing how they might react to this particular research method. Readers interested in this story can find resources at the end of this essay.

Mary and Susan have many important recommendations for those concerned with infants and toddlers. They note that caring for infants and toddlers requires both a strong knowledge base and the flexibility to respond to unique individuals who don't operate as a group and have less experience than older children in adjusting to the expectations of others. Two concepts they mentioned, continuity of care and primary caregiving, deserve definition. The goal of continuity of care is to increase the time that infants and toddlers spend with the same adults, people who come to know them well. This can be achieved by mixed-age groups, where babies enter when younger and stay until they move to a classroom for an older age group, resulting in a group of both infants and toddlers. Another strategy is to assign caregivers to a group of young babies, who then stay with them across time until they are ready to move into that older age group.

In primary caregiving each child is assigned a specific caregiver. This person is largely responsible for several tasks, including record-keeping of children's development, serving as a main resource for the family, and meeting the child's needs during routine caregiving such as diapering, feeding, and/or nap time. All caregivers remain involved with all of the children, but the goal is that one person for each child serves a central role.

The early childhood field embraces a mission of both care and education. Uniquely, with infants and toddlers, care is a predominant activity, and education is more fittingly informal learning resulting from babies exploring and striving to understand their worlds. Caring for babies overlaps with what is called childrearing in families. What babies are learning is not the same sort of content knowledge that makes up formal schooling. It is the task of infants and toddlers to learn an incredible number of words and what they signify, to test out what happens when they take action, and to form the relationships that will support their daily lives.

Susan and Mary brought the concept of rights to our attention, both the rights of families to high-quality programs and the rights of babies to excellent programs in which they can live their lives in a full and engaged way. Both contributors make clear how seriously they take their work, how much they respect our youngest children, and how passionate they are about improving the lives of babies and their families. This is serious, and personal, business for them, countering the degree to which this area of early childhood has so often been undervalued.

QUESTIONS FOR DISCUSSION

1. Families often experience a great deal of frustration and anxiety around finding suitable care for their infants and toddlers. How can this situation be changed?
2. In quality care, babies would have "a good day." What might a good day look like for an infant? A toddler?
3. The contributors raise the idea of children's rights. What rights should babies have in our society?

FOR FURTHER READING

Belsky, J. (1986). Infant day care: A cause for concern? *Zero to Three, 7,* 1–7.

Chazan-Cohen, R., Zaslow, M., Raikes, H. H., Elicker, J., Paulsell, D., Dean, A., & Kriener-Althen, K. (2017). *Working toward a definition of infant/toddler curricula: Intentionally furthering the development of individual children within responsive relationships.* Brief prepared for the Office of Planning, Research and Evaluation, Administration for Children and Families, U.S. Department of Health and Human Services.

Degotardi, S., & Pearson, E. (2014). *The relationship worlds of infants and toddlers: Multiple perspectives from early years theory and practice.* Open University Press.

Fein, G. G., & Fox, N. (Eds.). (1988). Infant day care: A special issue. *Early Childhood Research Quarterly, 3*(3).

Horm, D., Norris, D., Perry, D., Chazan-Cohen, R., & Halle, T. (2016). *Developmental foundations of school readiness for infants and toddlers: A research to practice report.* OPRE Report # 2016-07, Washington, DC: Office of Planning, Research and Evaluation, Administration for Children and Families, U.S. Department of Health and Human Services.

Howard, S. J., Mailk, R., Workman, S., & Hamm, K. (2018). *Understanding infant and toddler child care deserts.* Retrieved from https://www.americanprogress.org/wp-content/uploads/2018/10/IT-ChildCare-Deserts-13.pdf

Lally, R. J. (2013). *For our babies: Ending the invisible neglect of America's infants.* Teachers College Press.

McMullen, M. B. (2018). The many benefits of continuity of care for infants, toddlers, families, and caregiving staff. *Young Children, 73*(3), 38–39.

NICHD Early Care Research Network. (2002). Early child care and children's development prior to school entry: Results from the NICHD study of early child care. *American Educational Research Journal, 39*, 133–164.

Recchia, S. L., & Fincham, E. N. (2019) The significance of infant/toddler care and education. In C. P. Brown, M. B. McMullen, & N. File (Eds.), *The Wiley handbook of early care and education* (pp. 197–218). Wiley.

CHAPTER 7

Families and Family Engagement in Early Childhood Education

Douglas R. Powell and Mari Riojas-Cortez

Douglas R. Powell is Distinguished Professor Emeritus of Child Development and Family Studies at Purdue University. Prior to his 35 years at Purdue, he was on the faculty at Wayne State University and the Merrill-Palmer Institute in Detroit, Michigan. Beginning in the mid-1970s, his research and program development efforts focused on relations between families and schools, including early childhood programs. For more than a decade, he and Purdue colleague Karen E. Diamond conducted research on effects of technologically mediated supports for early childhood educators regarding children's literacy and language development. He led the development of the Early Learning Matters curriculum for the U.S. Department of Defense Child Development Program. He is former editor of the *Early Childhood Research Quarterly* and author of numerous research publications and integrative reviews of ECE research. Powell is a recipient of the Distinguished Contributions Award from the American Educational Research Association's Early Education and Child Development Group.

Mari Riojas-Cortez is Professor and Chair of the Early Childhood Studies Program at California State University Channel Islands. She received her Ph.D. from The University of Texas at Austin in Curriculum & Instruction with a concentration in Early Childhood Education and Multilingual Studies. Her research focuses on Latino family partnerships, children's play in dual-language settings, and early childhood teacher education. Dr. Riojas-Cortez's experience with early childhood settings began in San Antonio, Texas, as a prekindergarten bilingual teacher. Dr. Riojas-Cortez received the Outstanding Early Childhood Teacher Educator Award in 2019 from the National

Association of Early Childhood Teacher Educators and was selected as an Exchange Leader by the Exchange Leadership Initiative sponsored by Childcare Exchange. She served as the editor for *Dimensions of Early Childhood Journal* for 7 years. Currently, Dr. Riojas-Cortez serves on the editorial board for the *Journal of Early Childhood Teacher Education* and the *Early Childhood Education Journal*.

HOW HAVE IMAGES OF WHAT CONSTITUTES "FAMILY" CHANGED OVER THE COURSE OF YOUR CAREER?

DOUG: The concept of family was undergoing significant change when I entered the field in the early 1970s. The rapid growth of women in the workforce was a serious challenge to the assumption of a stay-at-home mother inherent in the long-dominant image of family. The idea of family that prevailed in the 1950s and 1960s was prominently represented on television in the popular *Leave It to Beaver* situation comedy series. Family meant mother as homemaker and primary child care provider; father as breadwinner and family decision-maker; typically developing biological children; white; and middle-class. These characteristics of family were—and to a lesser extent in some communities still are—the benchmark for determining the appropriateness of other types of families and programs designed to support families.

The idea of mothers in the paid workforce and young children in the care of nonfamilial others was a violation of societal norms that led to divisiveness within extended families and communities as well as among policymakers. Early childhood educators of my generation remember well the 1971 defeat of the nation's first comprehensive child development bill, which would have created a national day care system in support of working parents. In vetoing the legislation, President Richard Nixon claimed that the initiative would have promoted a "communal approach" to childrearing. Over time there has been greater acknowledgment and growing acceptance of families with mothers who work outside the home, though not to a threshold that embraces major improvements in federal support for early childhood programs.

Importantly, images of family have changed across the past 50 years to include, and sometimes celebrate, a range of trends in family life: single parenthood; racial, ethnic, and economic diversity; developmental differences across children; fathers' direct and sustained engagement of children's care; families headed by a gay/lesbian parent(s); co-parenting in situations of divorce or separation; and grandparents with primary or sole responsibility for rearing grandchildren. Professional standards essentially call for early childhood educators in today's world to simultaneously embrace multiple images of family. The extent to which this expectation is accepted and implemented is a complex "looking forward" matter.

MARI: I had to deeply reflect on the question regarding how the image of family has changed over the course of my career. My first intention was to think about families in the academic context and follow the chronological progression that we often cover in our early childhood textbooks and, of course, television shows of the 1960s and 1970s, even the census definition! Although I am very aware of the typical definitions of "family," my experience has given me the opportunity to know what constitutes a family in the context of minoritized populations such as Latinos. Working as a bilingual prekindergarten teacher in South Central Texas teaching Latino children in the 1980s, my image of family was different. The families that I worked with had very little in common (if anything) with the families from television shows and, certainly, our textbooks. Many *familias* (families) tended to watch shows on the Spanish TV station where *telenovelas* (soap operas) were the norm. The plot of the *telenovelas* always revolved around a family. Their trials and tribulations were for entertainment but not necessarily something to desire to be. These families were of different structures with very strong cultural values. Their funds of knowledge were eminent in everything they did for their children regardless of who was raising the children or who was in their family. Grandparents often took the role of primary caregiver, and friends would help parents, particularly single parents, with their children.

Unfortunately, the families that I worked with would often be depicted from a deficit perspective using terms such as "culturally disadvantaged" or "at risk" because they didn't fit the white middle-class characteristics. I think this is still the case for many minoritized populations such as Blacks, Latinos, Asians, and Native Americans (and others). The difference is the sense of agency that these minoritized groups have to discuss issues of race and discrimination as we hear more about anti-bias and antiracist early childhood education.

The image of the diversity of families has always been present, but we must acknowledge that this has not been a topic of discussion, particularly as it relates to race and ethnicity. Historically, minoritized families have not been given the respect they deserve, particularly in the way they are portrayed by the media and even by early childhood educators. The same is true for LGBTQIA+ families and immigrant families. I agree that professional standards call for early childhood educators to be committed to families, but the commitment also calls for positive and professional dispositions regarding the image of families. The professional disposition toward the images of families is a complex issue. To make matters even more difficult, the influence of social media like TikTok and Instagram and streaming services such as Hulu and Netflix is evident in the way that families are portrayed, and this influence largely affects the dispositions of early childhood educators.

DOUG: Your insights help us recognize that there are at least two ways to respond to the question of how images of what constitutes family have changed over the course of our careers: (1) images set forth in professional literature, policies, and mass media, and (2) individual understandings we construct through direct, sustained interactions with families. Like you, I found that these two information sources can yield different, often conflicting images of family.

In the late 1970s, I led a neighborhood-based program in a Detroit suburb that offered twice-weekly peer-support group discussions for parents (mostly mothers) of infants and toddlers, plus an early education classroom for preschool-age children of participating families. Most families had roots in Appalachia, especially Kentucky and Tennessee, and had moved to the Detroit area for work in industries that manufactured parts for automobile companies. The families in the neighborhood—not the program's families only—were not part of the dramatic increase in women working outside the home. Traditional mother and father roles seemed very much entrenched, although I recall some reports of group discussions in which women shared stories of how to increase their use of the sole family vehicle. Whether boys should be allowed to play with the dolls the program initially provided in the preschool classroom emerged as a major controversy and focus of tense negotiations with the preschool teachers.

In my initial response to our question, I carefully chose several key words (now in boldface) in the following sentence: "Importantly, images of family have changed across the past 50 years to *include*, and sometimes *celebrate*, a range of trends in family life. . . ." I deeply regretted opting for the word "include" instead of a more positive term, such as "accept" or "embrace," and using the word "sometimes" to qualify our celebration of different family forms and lifestyles. The basis of my deep regret, of course, is the deficit perspective that you appropriately describe as alive and well in the labels our field often uses to depict families that differ from white, middle-class characteristics. Terminology such as "disadvantaged" is powerful. I urge our readers to reflect on the significance of your use of the word "minoritized."

I am learning through our exchange here that responding to the question about changes over time in images of families is also an on-ramp to our later consideration of professional dispositions and behaviors as well as program policies and practices. I am thankful for our opportunity to look first at the images of family that prevail in our field. What more would you like to add to the foundation we are building for our chapter on families?

MARI: It is evident that the images of families have evolved in the last 50+ years. What I appreciated from your response was the focus on the terms that we use as we discuss families, because words create images. For example, I used the term "minoritized" rather than "minority" to exemplify those groups that have been historically marginalized as opposed to "minority," as it has a different connotation that promotes deficit thinking. Using appropriate terminology allows us to change the images of families in the present. As I continue to work with future early childhood teachers, I can see the diversity in their lives and how images of the past inform what it used to be, but not the currently lived reality.

COVID also changed the images of families, as it claimed so many lives. Families had to take care of one another and welcome one another's children. The children had to adapt to new families who may or may not be related and who may be of different structure and style. We need to continue the discussion of the images of families because families, just like culture, are dynamic, always changing and evolving.

HOW HAS THE ROLE OF FAMILIES AND FAMILY ENGAGEMENT IN SCHOOLS CHANGED OVER THE COURSE OF YOUR CAREER?

MARI: Technology, COVID, racial inequities, and mental health are all issues that have impacted the role of the families in the last 30 years. The role of the family has often been through the parent lens and may include the following: provider; protector; nurturer; comforter; counselor; motivator; and many others. As I think of the role of families and family engagement, I must think about my personal experience, because our experiences influence our perspectives. The role of the families has changed somewhat throughout the course of my career.

I grew up in a family where the focus was to provide basic needs while providing love, affection, care, support, and laughter. Although resources were limited, my parents always made sure we had food and shelter. The families that I worked with when I was a bilingual prekindergarten teacher in a public school in Texas shared similar values and experiences. I come from a working-class immigrant family where my father and my mother only had a few years of primary schooling and did not speak English; the families that I worked with shared a similar experience.

The school where I worked in the late 1980s emphasized the importance of the family in a child's life as teachers. We made sure that we made connections from the time the parents enrolled their children until we saw them transition to larger elementary schools. We knew that the families that we worked with provided basic needs along with love, support, and motivation. This was evident daily as the families took the children to "*la escuelita*" every day. Education was very important for these families because their role was to ensure that the children not only attended school but were "*bien educados*" (well-educated/mannered). Parents engaged with the school for support. In essence, their role was to support their children. The families' role seemed to evolve as they became partners with us in their children's development and learning.

At that time, the term "funds of knowledge" had not been introduced in professional training or university courses, but somehow as teachers we understood the critical influence of the home for children's learning and development. We knew that children learned at home. I recall the wealth of knowledge I gained regarding the role of the families as I visited their homes at the beginning of each school year. What I noticed the most was the love that the families had for their children and the importance of supporting them as they went to prekindergarten, which was not (and still not) compulsory. Thus, the role of the family largely depends on their cultural practices.

In speaking recently with an undergraduate student, first-gen, Latinx immigrant, mother of two young children, it was evident that her perspective of her role as a parent was different than her mother's. This student mentioned that her mother saw herself as a provider, making sure that the children were fed and clean. She saw her mother as a strong woman who was determined to provide for her children.

In contrast, this student sees herself differently than her mother. Her role is not only to provide for the children together with her husband but also to nurture, guide, and motivate them.

Just as families have evolved over time, so has the concept of "family engagement." The terms that are often used regarding family engagement have also evolved. We used to use the term *parent involvement,* and this evolved to *family engagement,* then *family partnerships,* and most recently *family learning.* These terms help us to understand how our notions regarding the family's role in children's learning and development have also changed. Moll's "Funds of Knowledge" framework [published in *Theory into Practice* in 1992] is key to understanding how cultural practices relate to different roles and types of engagement that families have with their children. Similarly, Joyce Epstein's "Framework of the Six Types of Family Involvement" has been instrumental in understanding how families navigate the world of engagement in schools where they are often misunderstood.

DOUG: I take special note of your description of the wealth of knowledge about families that you learned during home visits at the beginning of the school year. I think your approach to home visits represents a paradigm shift that was in its early stages of adoption when I entered the field in the early 1970s. Your sensitivity to family cultural practices, including love and support for a child's participation in a preschool program, speaks to an openness to and acceptance of differences in childrearing that, in my view, are the basis of responsiveness in home-school relationships.

I would welcome a description or example of how the knowledge you learned during a home visit informed your work with a child and your relationship with the child's parent(s) or family. I ask because I believe our field continues to need good illustrations of home–school partnerships at the individualized level of a teacher's connections with child, parent, and family. So much of the "programming" featured in the professional literature on home–school relationships approaches parents as a group, often disconnected from their children, and in an episodic nature that highlights events, such as a back-to-school orientation meeting, rather than an evolving, ongoing, and dynamic set of interactions between parent/family/child and teacher/classroom.

Early in my career, I was exposed to some methods of family engagement that were implicitly based on an "expert-knows-best" perspective. In a home visit conducted within this framework, the expert would use an informal or formal set of criteria to determine the quality of the family environment. Perceived weaknesses, such as a small number of books readily available for the child, would be used to prescribe actions in the home and/or school to improve supports for a child's learning and development. Critics of this compensatory approach to education viewed it as a deficit model of family engagement. For certain, it has the potential to foster biases related to class, race, ethnicity, ability, and other meaningful differences.

My early work with families with young children attempted to shift the source of childrearing information from experts to other families through the use of small support groups of parents (mostly mothers). I mentioned this neighborhood-based program earlier. I'd like to share more about a family engagement approach that emphasizes parent support versus the narrower lens of parent education. But first, I will pause as an opportunity for you to expand on your uses of the funds of knowledge about family cultural practices, if you wish.

MARI: In order to create partnerships, you have to develop relationships. A relationship is created when two individuals (or more) learn about each other. Home visits did that for me as a new teacher. There are so many examples of the funds of knowledge that I learned from the families on the south side of San Antonio during home visits. Home visits helped me not only to learn about the families, but I was also able to build and establish trust because they also learned more about me. I, however, was not alone during those home visits; the paraprofessional assigned to my classroom came with me. We became a team. This colleague was a very valuable resource because she knew the community well. As we drove up to the homes, we talked about how we would greet the family and the length of time that we needed to stay. We often stayed longer because of the conversations we had with the parents, mostly the mothers. Most of the fathers were at work, and in some cases the mother was on her own or had other family members living with them. The families always made us feel welcome as they greeted us inside their homes. After every home visit we learned how much they appreciated "*que las maestras los visitaran en su hogar*" (that the teachers visited them in their home). The funds of knowledge represented here was the appreciation for teachers and the value of conversations. Another example of funds of knowledge was the importance of "*compartir,*" or sharing, even when you don't have much. The families that we visited had very limited resources, but everyone had something they wanted to "*compartir,*" and they would not take no for an answer. Not accepting their gift would have been considered a "*grosería*" or rudeness. Some families shared *pan dulce* (sweet bread), coffee, fruit, flowers; we even had one family who shared some beautiful clay cups from Mexico. We experienced their funds of knowledge not only during our home visits but throughout the school year, as families were always ready to share not only for classroom activities but also for my own personal needs. I remember one year one of the mothers found out that my father had been diagnosed with diabetes and she wanted to help. This mother brought me *nopalitos* [vegetable dish] because she wanted to make sure I knew the importance of nopalitos as a good source of fiber for diabetics, and most importantly she valued my father as an elder (another example of funds of knowledge). The home visits helped me know about the value of taking care of the elders, taking care of plants and animals, and the importance of the family as a unit.

Collectively I experienced how families cared for their children's well-being, which was evident as the families ensured that their children came to school on time and prepared. As the families dropped off their children, they gave them "*consejos*," which is so much more than advice. *Consejos* were intertwined with the good-byes as a loving reminder of the value families placed on the concept of education. These *consejos* were of value because I had the opportunity to see children using them, such as "*escucha a tu maestra*"(listen to your teacher), "*te portas bien*" (be well-mannered), "*no llores, al ratito vengo*" (don't cry, I will be right back), "*le ayudas a tu maestra*" (help your teacher). As you can see, these are more than just advice; these are the cultural values that help children thrive in their daily lives including school. I often asked about specific *consejos* during circle time to give children agency about their funds of knowledge. I remember the children having a conversation about crying in school because we had two children who would cry. They would tell the two children, Lionel and Amanda, "*no llores ahorita, viene tu mamá* (don't cry, your mom is coming)," which is the *consejo* that Amanda's mother would always tell her before leaving. As we talked in circle time, we learned that Amanda would cry because her mother was pregnant and she knew that at some point her mother would go to the hospital, but Amanda didn't want to be without her. The conversation allowed for children to share their thoughts and worries, and although we did not solve Amanda's crying, she knew she could talk about it during circle time or any time and we would listen. I would also often hear the children talk about crying as they played in the learning centers, particularly in the housekeeping center or dramatic play. They also liked to converse with one another in the art center, and as they talked, they would engage in creative creations, particularly with play dough. My classroom became a context where children could learn about one another, a place that represented their values and honored their funds of knowledge. As I reflect on my practices as a teacher, I realize the importance of learning from families and the families learning about me as a person, not only as a teacher. This type of learning allowed me to create relationships based on mutual respect and trust.

I agree that we need to move away from the parent education model or approach. I think parent education comes from a deficit perspective. I like the idea of family support and family learning. I look forward to learning more about the family engagement approach you mentioned.

DOUG: There are many conceptual links between the examples of your approach to working with families and the neighborhood-based program I established and coordinated decades ago involving families with infants. The program emphasized parent support, especially among small groups of parents, and fostered learning about child development through families' shared knowledge of and experiences with childrearing. As in your work, the quality of interpersonal relationships was central to the program's viability. Self-disclosure is fully dependent on the perceived trustworthiness and authenticity of the listener. To that end, the small, long-term parent groups in our program were facilitated by individuals from the community who had backgrounds and life experiences similar to the parent participants. We thought of the group facilitators as "near peers." They used open-ended questions to initiate group conversations (e.g., What do you remember about your first days at home with your baby?) and built on participants' comments to promote discussion. The group facilitators, all paraprofessionals, were supported by a highly experienced and credentialed early childhood teacher.

We found that it was initially challenging for some participants to view their experiences as valuable to share with others in a peer-group discussion format. They wanted to "hear what an expert has to say." Over time, parents in the groups began to recognize the affirmations they received from telling their stories and the connections they made with other participants who reported similar experiences in parenting and child development. We informally observed that nearly all program parents viewed their pregnancy and childbirth (or adoption process) as fully unique, but wanted assurances that their child's development and their parenting feelings and experiences were "normal."

Topics pursued by the discussion groups were at the discretion of each group. At times, group facilitators felt challenged by the wide range of topics the participants pursued. In addition to basic child development interests, most groups also explored family interests, such as relations with the baby's grandparents, and topics related to the shared neighborhood context, such as disagreements with landlords and displeasure with the upkeep of the neighborhood's park. Several groups joined together to convene a program-wide meeting with city officials wherein parents vented their frustrations and made the case for better oversight of government regulations and practices, plus better access to publicly funded resources.

We have impressive anecdotal evidence that the program contributed to parents' confidence in the value of their childrearing experiences and the experiences of other parents. What is more, when their children entered school, they mobilized their collective wisdom to engage in reciprocal partnerships with their child's teacher and school administrators.

I am pleased that each of us responded to the question about family engagement with novel experiences that, at their core, demonstrate a commitment to parents and teachers developing relationships informed by learning from and respecting one another.

WHAT HAVE BEEN THE MOST IMPORTANT FACTORS IMPACTING HOW AND WHAT WE DO WITH FAMILIES AS ECE EDUCATORS?

DOUG: I am pleased that the editors focused our question on "most important" factors because this could be quite an expansive discussion. As a potential starting point, my thought is that important influences on our field's work with families fall into three broad and overlapping categories:

1. recent developments that are transforming how we live, including technological advances and the COVID pandemic you cited earlier;
2. prevailing practice traditions and beliefs in our field and the institutions that provide ECE; and
3. persistent, longer-term patterns in our society, including but not limited to the racial inequities that you also cited earlier.

Connections across these three areas and between factors are profound. We cannot discuss COVID-19 without considering racial, ethnic, and income differences in its devastation and treatment, for example. And in many settings, the COVID-19 pandemic seems to have significantly increased the use of technologically mediated communications between educators and families, perhaps with an emphasis on the parent education tradition in our field (e.g., activities to do with your child at home this week). Yet to look closely at what is impacting relationships between families and early childhood programs, I find it useful to attempt to unpack contexts into meaningful chunks, such as these three broad categories.

As indirectly suggested in my first paragraph, I would like to broaden the scope of the question, from ECE educators to the *field* of early childhood education. Educators carry out their work within an institutional system of values and practices that sometimes gets ignored in discussions that pinpoint educators. This is why I include practice traditions and beliefs as a major set of influences on family engagement. Early in our respective careers, the Texas school system where you taught devoted time to home visits, and the Michigan school system with which I collaborated for the neighborhood project anticipated benefits in connecting with parents of infants. If we push deeper here, there is a question of what factors led each of us to independently embrace a paradigm that emphasized careful listening and building relationships based on what we learn. What influences led us in this direction, and away from an expert-knows-best approach to working with families?

What do you think of the basic elements of this road map? Are there different paths you would like to pursue? The editors are inviting us to address a really challenging question!

MARI: This is a challenging question indeed! I appreciate how you are suggesting a new approach; I like the idea of a road map. A road map gives us directions, but it allows us to select which route to take. The three points that you made earlier are broad enough to guide us in a deep conversation, and I believe that these can be a model for others to follow in their own conversations. I will address my thoughts on each.

(1) Recent developments that are transforming how we live, including technological advances and the COVID pandemic.

Families were transformed by the pandemic in many ways. We heard tragic stories about how families lost many members of their immediate and extended family and how those losses greatly affected children. Other stories were about the increase in the number of families facing housing and food insecurities. Families had to move in together because they lost their homes. I recall a mother being interviewed as she was in line to get food from the food bank and feeling embarrassed that she had to ask for food, but she had lost her job and her husband's income was not enough. The disparities were more evident for vulnerable populations that had no access to outdoor environments and nature, something that these families, always face. Families with backyards were able to go outdoors, but those that lived in apartments, including public housing, did not have that privilege. Families with children who had special needs faced even more dire situations. For example, children on the autism spectrum and other intellectual challenges had a difficult time adjusting to a new reality. Although technology is often used with children with these types of disabilities, the virtual learning environment was indeed very restrictive. Furthermore, we know that technology was another factor that highlighted the disparities among marginalized populations and one that caused social and emotional stress for children and families.

(2) Prevailing practice traditions and beliefs in our field and the institutions that provide ECE.

Although there is a critical need to meet children's social and emotional stress inflicted by the pandemic and racial inequities, we still see the "business as usual" approach to family engagement. These approaches include workshops that are tailored to white, middle-class families, which miss the realities faced by many marginalized families. A shift in perspective is needed to meet the needs of the families we serve. I agree with you in that a new paradigm has to be created where we listen and get to know the families in order to—and I'll include your words—"build relationships based on what we learn." This type of thinking will help us shift away from "being the experts" to "being partners" through the practice of deep listening, which helps to build trust, empathy and *respeto mutuo* (mutual respect).

(3) Persistent, longer-term patterns in our society, including but not limited to the racial inequities.

There are persistent patterns in our society that impede the development of meaningful relationships with families. We see the prevalence of unconscious and explicit biases that are ingrained stereotypes and attitudes, particularly toward "the other," which often include racial differences but also age, gender, sexuality, religion, ability, language, and more. We as teacher educators must learn to decipher these biases that perpetuate in our schools and communities. We must work with our students to reflect on their own biases so that when they work with families, they are prepared to practice deep listening so that they can, in turn, learn more about families, which will help them build trust, empathy and *respeto* toward children and families.

WHAT FAMILY PERSPECTIVES/ENGAGEMENT DO WE NEED IN THE FUTURE?

MARI: In this chapter we have focused on historical perspectives of family engagement as well as major factors to consider about working with families. We had a great conversation presenting our experiences that together amount to almost 85 years in the field! What I appreciated the most from this conversation is the opportunity to reflect in a different way on our perspectives regarding family partnerships. Reflection is an important aspect as we continue to move the early childhood field forward.

As I reflect back on our conversation, I think we both agree on the need to think about family partnerships in a different way. We also discussed the possibility of creating a road map that will help us as we continue our work with families. A road map will give the early childhood field opportunities to define goals for family partnerships and should include milestones that are needed to reach those goals. The road map will help early childhood educators to think about why family partnerships are important. Then it will also assist with the work that has to be done to achieve family partnerships. Lastly, a timeline is important to ensure that this initiative is not forgotten.

The example that comes to mind as I think about a road map is one of a kindergarten teacher whom I will call Irma who wanted to increase families' participation in children's literacy development (the goal) in her classroom. This kindergarten teacher taught in a bilingual classroom. The two strategies that she used to achieve her goal included home visits and classroom visits (milestones). Although this teacher had experience working with families, she felt that visiting the children's home was the first milestone that needed to be met. She took about 3 weeks to visit most of her families, which gave her a different perspective about them. Irma learned that families were also interested in learning more about how to help their children learn to read and write. Basically, the families cared about their child's literacy development. After developing a timeline, Irma was able to reach the second milestone, which was the families' classroom visits. Irma brought the families to her classroom, which makes this a reciprocal experience. Just like she visited the families' homes, she opened up the opportunity for families to visit the classroom. Irma invited them to attend and share any stories they wanted to share. Based on her equity lens, she encouraged them to tell oral stories so that all families with diverse literacy experiences had the opportunity to share. Irma changed the context for early literacy learning several times with much success (remember the road map?). First, she invited families to bring their blankets and sit under a magnolia tree that was right outside her classroom. Although this was not a familiar early literacy experience (sometimes there are sharp turns on the road!) for many of her families, they welcomed it and happily participated. Second, Irma was able to take the families on a field trip to the local public library, where families learned about the process of obtaining a library card and checking out and returning books. Many families began to visit the public library on their own, thus helping their children engage in an early literacy experience. In my opinion, Irma reached her destination! The partnership created had a goal, but it took Irma some time to reach the destination because she first needed to learn more about the families and how to work together for a common goal.

From this example I see the importance of co-partnering. The teacher set the tone to create trust and *respeto,* and families felt comfortable to first participate and engage. As relationships developed, co-partnering became the focus. I truly like the term *co-partnering* because it helps us see families from an asset-based perspective, something we desperately need in our schools and centers.

DOUG: I also like the "co-partnering" term. One of its appealing attributes is that the "co" part of the term conveys a desired balance of power, responsibility, and information-sharing. The field of ECE has long used the phrase "parents as partners" to communicate an image of relationships between schools/teachers and families/parents. The word "partner" is ambiguous, however. It is open to interpretations that can lead to arrangements with senior and junior partners or maybe silent partners. The co-partnering term is also appealing because its "ing" ending connotes an active process rather than a fixed relationship.

In co-partnering, all parties have expertise to share. In your example involving Irma, parents received information and resources from their children's teacher on ways to promote their children's literacy. They also shared their literacy expertise by telling stories as part of an organized activity under a magnolia tree. Contrast this image with a more traditional classroom visit in which parents are invited to watch a teacher demonstrate how to read with children. Importantly, Irma's home visits helped her learn that parents wanted to know more about how to promote their child's reading and writing abilities. Irma and the parents of the children in her room had common ground.

My hunch is that the road map Irma constructed with parents underwent further development after she met her home and classroom visit milestones. As I noted early in our conversation, family engagement is ideally an ongoing relationship, not a set of events. New opportunities to work together on behalf of children naturally emerge when teachers and families are tuned into each other. I can easily imagine a parent saying, "Let's make a classroom picture book of our family stories" at the conclusion of the magnolia tree gathering.

I strongly concur that trust and *respeto* are essential to co-partnering. My experiences in ECE consistently support this view. Research I conducted with Nancy File and colleagues also indicates that parent views of their child's teacher's *responsiveness* to their child and family is a key component of effective parent-teacher relationships in ECE. Helping teachers initiate and foster respectful connections with the families of children in their classrooms seems central to moving forward with family engagement in our field.

MARI: I recently had a conversation with an administrator from a school district about how the pandemic had affected the relationship with families and that it was important to "bring the parents back" [to school], but it was also important to find ways for teachers to "want the parents back." This situation reminded me of teachers' dispositions and the influence they have on family partnerships. I think this brings us to the importance of teachers' dispositions for initiating respectful relationships. Positive teacher's dispositions often show a higher level of family engagement and, thus, possibilities not only for partnerships but most importantly for co-partnering.

If we reflect back on Irma, we can see how she initiated gaining trust and thus *respeto* from the parents. It is obvious that Irma had very positive dispositions toward families. Her tenacity in building relationships showed in the home visits and the other early literacy related events that she planned. The planning involved in-depth communication and conversations, something that families appreciate from teachers. I also think that she had to have empathy for all and any situations that families were facing that may have prevented them from fully participating in the early literacy events. Initiating partnerships is not an easy task, but it can be done through effective reflection, an action plan, and positive dispositions.

But teachers are only one part of the story in co-partnering. The other part of the story are the families. I would like to address a statement you made about "parent views of their child's teacher's *responsiveness* to their child and family." We have to divide this statement into two parts. First, we need to know the "parent views of their child's teacher." It is important to know and understand the families' perspective of the teacher. Teachers may be more concerned with colleagues' or administrators' perspectives, but not too much with families'. Those teachers with negative or challenging dispositions may not think that the way a family sees them is relevant or even important. Working through those challenging dispositions becomes a must. The second part is very significant, ". . . teacher's *responsiveness* to their child and family." This tells us that the families' perception is based on how the teacher responds or treats their child, which takes us back to trust and *respeto*. I appreciate the analysis you provided of the word "co-partnering," as it not only provides a broad definition but also reflection. Relationships are built on trust and *respeto*, and we must prepare teachers to work on their dispositions for successful co-partnering.

DOUG: Supporting teachers to engage in respectful and trustful relationships with families will undoubtedly require attention to a teacher's approach to the issues of diversity we discussed at the beginning of our conversation. Negative and/or stereotyped views of members of a minoritized community or a parent of a child whose race or ethnicity differs from that of the parent's, for example, are likely to impact the quality of co-partnering. My experience is that an individualized strategy of support may be especially productive here. I recall observing a fruitful exchange between a teacher and a supervisor when the supervisor thoughtfully invited the teacher to unpack the word "but" in the teacher's comment, "The parent is gay but seems to spend time with the kid."

Encouraging parents to engage in co-partnering with their child's teacher can involve its own set of challenges. Some of the barriers here may include stressful life circumstances that afford limited time for meaningful connections with a teacher and their child's classroom, lingering consequences of prior negative experiences with schools or teachers, and perhaps a view of the program or teacher as a purchased or public service provider (e.g., presenting the teacher with a list of curriculum activities to implement with their child during the week). In my view, teachers are in a strong position to set the stage for co-partnering relationships by understanding and respecting where each family is. And this process cannot happen until teachers "want the parents back," as your administrator colleague so aptly put it.

Our earlier conversation about factors that impact what ECE educators do with families is a strong reminder that our field cannot expect teachers to initiate and nurture co-partnering relationships with families on their own. At a minimum, educators need a guiding framework for thinking about families, such as NAEYC's position statement on developmentally appropriate practice; pre- and inservice professional development on families and family engagement that includes concrete illustrations of practice options and constructive feedback on their own practices; tangible support from administrators and educator colleagues; time in their workday to connect and plan with families; and forums for sharing their professional experiences with other educators. To adapt a well-regarded understanding in our field, it takes a village for educators and families to engage in co-partnering.

Reflections on the Families and Family Engagement in Early Childhood Education Conversation

Andrew J. Stremmel

The concept of family and how we think about the role of families has undergone significant change over the last 50-plus years. What has not changed is the crucial importance of the family for children's learning and development. The family is the first and primary source of influence on children's development, and, as Doug Powell and Mari Riojas-Cortez make abundantly clear, it is the role of early childhood educators to find ways to help families create home environments that support learning, while at the same time listening to parents for ideas on ways educators can create a school environment that encourages and supports family strengths and potential. Doug and Mari both emphasize that trusting, caring relationships with parents are the basis from which to construct educational experiences with children.

Mari notes that while the image of the diversity of families has always been present, it has not been part of the dominant narrative about families. The notion of the traditional family (male provider, female housewife, and several children) depicted in popular television shows of the 1950s and 1960s, and even in our professional literature, represents an idealized image of families that is at odds with findings on the history of the family (see Coontz, 1992). This image of families does not portray how most Americans lived and has little in common with the experience of many marginalized, particularly ethnically and racially diverse, families.

Moreover, although the view of parents as the child's first teacher still prevails, parents from minoritized groups (those groups that have been historically marginalized) have not had the same influence with teachers and schools as have white, middle-class parents, and have largely been viewed from a deficit perspective. This has created the misconception (or preconception) that parents from minoritized groups are less caring or interested in their children's learning. However, solid evidence exists to suggest that all parents want what is best for their children, including a high-quality education (Gonzalez et al., 2005; Tobin et al., 2013). All parents want to support their children in being successful academically and in life, and all parents need support and encouragement for their childrearing practices. The key is how to successfully link families and schools.

In early childhood education, we have seen a tremendous shift in thinking about parents as needing to be educated toward being seen as partners. And this requires a further shift in thinking about what parent partnership really means. Doug points out that the term "parents as partners" often has communicated an image of unequal relationships between home and school, one that only sees the school/teacher as expert. That is, traditional approaches to parent education and involvement involved one-directional interactions that have not been conducive to building positive, meaningful relationships based on what can be learned from and about families. This can be seen in cases where parents are contacted only when there is a problem or when there is a need for some kind of assistance, perhaps as volunteers to go on a field trip or read to children in the classroom. These forms of "parent partnerships" may be useful to the teacher, but they do not often create the conditions for meaningful exchange that, for example, enable parents to find out what is going on in the classroom, or be a regular source of information about their child that may influence change in what teachers do.

Moll's "funds of knowledge" approach (see González et al., 2005) seems key to countering deficit thinking and understanding how cultural practices relate to different roles and types of engagement that families have with their children. According to this approach, minoritized families have linguistic and cultural resources, extensive knowledge and abilities based on their daily practices and lived experiences (accumulated funds of knowledge) that can be employed to support children's learning in school. In this approach, parents are not just willing consumers of child development knowledge that is generated and disseminated by scholars and educators; parents are a powerful and important source of knowledge about children. As partners, teachers and families learn about and share their knowledge of child development as they exchange views, experiences, and expertise. Recognizing that parents can contribute knowledge, ideas, and skills that they alone have of their children acknowledges parents as competent and authentic chroniclers of their families' experiences, values, and beliefs.

Doug and Mari share stories from their experiences of working with families that, at their core, demonstrate a commitment to parents and teachers developing relationships informed by learning from and respecting one another. Their use of home visits, small parent support groups, and activities that foster dialogue between teachers and families provided opportunities for families to be recognized, respected, and heard, stemming from a belief that parents are equal stakeholders (co-partners) in supporting children's learning and development and family well-being. Doug and Mari suggest that the term "co-partnering" will help educators to view families from an asset-based perspective. Seeing families at promise means honoring and understanding who families are, where they come from, and what their capabilities are, and creating opportunities for families to share their culture and to participate fully in the discussion of what is in their child's best interest. Family engagement values and supports parent interaction and participation as a means of strengthening the enduring relationship between parent and child. For educators, this should always be our foremost goal.

QUESTIONS FOR DISCUSSION

1. In discussing the influences that led them away from an "expert-knows-best" approach to working with families in a way that emphasized careful listening and building relationships, the authors point to connections across broad areas that include technological advances, the pandemic, predominant practice traditions and beliefs in our field, and persistent patterns in our society (including explicit biases and racial inequities) that hinder the development of meaningful relationships with families. How have these influences impacted your thinking and/or practices in working with families?
2. What are some of the ways early childhood educators can seek out and recognize opportunities to listen to families at this current moment in time? Can we listen in a way that really matters or makes a difference?

3. Based on what you read in this chapter and from your own experiences, what are some ways parents and teachers can support each other's roles in the child's development?

FOR FURTHER READING

Castro, D., Bryant, D. M., Peisner-Feinberg, E. S., & Skinner, M. L. (2004). Parent involvement in Head Start programs: The role of parent, teacher, and classroom characteristics. *Early Childhood Research Quarterly, 19,* 413–430.

Coontz, S. (1992). *The way we never were: American families and the nostalgia trap.* New York: Basic Books.

Epstein, J. L., & Sanders, M. G. (2002). Family, school, and community partnerships. In M. Bornstein (Ed.), *Handbook of parenting: Vol. 5. 2nd ed. Practical issues in parenting* (pp. 407–437) Erlbaum.

González, N., Moll, L. C., & Amanti, C. (2005). *Funds of knowledge: Theorizing practices in households, communities, and classrooms.* New York: Routledge.

Powell, D. R. (2001). Visions and realities of achieving partnership: Parent–school relationships at the turn of the century. In A. Göncü & E. Klein (Eds.), *Children in play, story and school* (pp. 333–357). New York: Guilford.

Powell, D. R., Son, S., File, N., & San Juan, R. R. (2010). Parent–school relationships and children's academic and social outcomes in public school pre-kindergarten. *Journal of School Psychology, 48*, 269–292.

Riojas-Cortez, M., & Flores, B. B. (2009). Supporting preschoolers' social development in schools through funds of knowledge. *Journal of Early Childhood Research*, 7(2), 187–201.

Tobin, J., Arzubiaga, A. E., &Adair, J. K. (2013). *Children crossing borders.* Russell Sage Foundation.

CHAPTER 8

Closing Thoughts

Reflections and (Re)Claiming

Katherine K. Delaney

Katherine K. Delaney is an Associate Professor of Early Childhood Education at the University of Toledo in Toledo, Ohio, where she teaches and learns from preservice teachers; practicing teachers; and district, early childhood, and Head Start program leaders. Kate's research focuses on how local, state, and federal policies impact the lived experiences of teachers, children, and families in early childhood spaces. Kate also works with local early childhood providers, teachers, and agencies to advocate for expanded and inclusive care for young children. Prior to becoming a teacher educator and researcher, Kate was a preschool teacher in New York City and Milwaukee, Wisconsin.

Across the chapters in this book, impactful and innovative contributors in the field have shared their lived experiences conducting early childhood research, working with families, leading agencies, supporting providers, and informing the work of policymakers. Their work has been foundational in informing the ways I approached practices in my preschool classroom when I was a teacher, in what I teach students in my university's pre-K-to-5th-grade teacher education program, and how my doctoral students and I ground our research designs and analyses. It was deeply interesting to me to hear these important contributors reflect on what mattered the most in their professional careers, how their views and ways of working changed over time, and what they identified as key areas of focus for our ECE field moving forward. I was particularly struck by the ways in which the pairings of the authors resulted in challenging, contradictory, and enriching conversations about the seminal research and practices in our field across the past 30 years. It is safe to say that for all of us, our lived experiences in the world, our backgrounds (families and communities), and our identities inform how we engage with children and families. Who we are is central to who we are with children.

As a scholar in the middle of my career, I often find myself speaking with my own students about what has been accomplished in our field, and how they hope to contribute to our field's knowledge through their own work. These conversations about what they view as needing the field's attention have been deeply important to my own work and ways of thinking. My students are a mix of preservice teacher candidates, seeking to work in pre-K-through-5th-grade classrooms; master's degree students, many of whom work in infant, toddler and preschool classrooms in community-based settings; and doctoral students who hope to contribute to the field through research, teacher education and leadership. Their experiences and views of what must happen next for ECE to continue progressing have been deeply influential on the choices I make about what I can and do contribute through my research, teaching, and service efforts. To prepare for this chapter, I asked four of my students to tell me how they feel about the future of ECE and their perspectives on what needs to happen in the future. These were their responses:

> The future of ECE is very grim without substantial investments coupled with targeted policy changes that will support the child care workforce. Teachers can't afford to stay in the field due to shockingly low wages, and parents cannot shoulder the burden of rising costs for child care. Market-based solutions do not work for education. We must view child care like K–12, a public good, and it must be funded similarly.

> The future of ECE depends on a changing mindset about what young children really need, not what we need from them. We need to prioritize early childhood education as a fundamental right and fund ECE accordingly.

> When we talk about children's social and emotional well-being and their academic learning, I sometimes feel like I am trying to merge together two things that just don't go together very easily. When I'm in my classroom, children's well-being always leads, but it also makes me worry that I won't get there where they need to be before I send them to kindergarten.

> Everyone gives me a hard time about wanting to become a teacher. They think I'm crazy. But it's really the only thing I've ever wanted to be. I hope

> that things change with this intense focus on kids reading by the end of kindergarten. It's hard to watch my cooperating teacher and her students struggle and feel behind already in 1st grade. I didn't really think 1st-graders could be stressed out, but they are. A lot.

What struck me first about their responses is how grounded their visions of the future of ECE are in the lived experiences of early care professionals, young children, and their families. They see the children and families they work with, and understand that the current system is not tenable, and that they must be a part of making that change. They also do not shy away from the realities of the present-day challenges for our field.

Honestly, when I started my Ph.D. in 2008, I was riding the tide of President Obama's election and the rising visibility of public pre-kindergarten funding. President Obama was quoting the work of Dr. James Heckman, an economist, about the power of early childhood investments, Congress was rallying behind pre-kindergarten, and it seemed like we finally had an argument (investment equals positive outcomes for life!) that had caught the attention of the American people more than any past Abecedarian or Head Start study. I remember feeling a little worried about thinking of children as economic units of investment. The idea that we should invest in children because of who they could be, or what they could contribute in the future, was both engaging to the public, and troubling to those working with children and families who saw their lived experiences as reason enough to invest in responsive and supportive early care and learning environments.

But I was also very excited about the prospect of pre-kindergarten opportunities for all children. As so many of us did, I viewed these promises without much consideration of unintended consequences. Early childhood as a rallying cry and a field worthy of attention and investment had finally arrived!

In my doctoral coursework, we did talk about how this investment approach might backfire if studies didn't show what we hoped they would. That being said, the federal investment in research on the impacts of pre-kindergarten paid for my doctoral education, and it put me in classrooms with children and teachers and sparked my lifelong interest in how teachers and children make decisions about external local, state, and federal requirements.

It's hard to believe that in the 10-plus years since that speech was made, and the explosion of publicly funded pre-kindergarten on the public scene, so very much has changed once again. In contrast, my students are entering the field as the next generation of teachers, policymakers, agency leaders, and researchers, stepping into a country, and early childhood system, reeling from years of turmoil due to divestment, political strife, and a global pandemic. We face a child care crisis, a workforce crisis, and a reduction of federal and state investments in ECE. In the local communities in which I work, early care professionals struggle with high turnover and low wages, challenging work environments, limited resources, and limited support. Families in desperate need of responsive, caring settings for their children, especially those with special needs and/or disabilities, struggle to find it. The system feels held together by tape and paper clips. And yet, every semester, students come into our program eager and willing to support the needs of children and families, despite the challenges they observe and engage with. I find myself deeply heartened by their commitment to understanding the diverse needs of learners and their families, the ways in which they foreground children's social and emotional needs, and their commitment to open and inclusive practices that welcome all identities and persons.

As these soon-to-be early childhood teacher educators/researchers note in their responses to my questions, the challenges seem larger, the resources scarcer, and the solutions further from reach. It helps me understand my students' skepticism. Even though we have learned so much through research about what young children need to be supported successfully, we have yet to gather the popular and political will in the United States, and many places around the world, to meet these needs. In reading the conversations in the chapters, and reflecting on what the editors have asked me to do in this chapter, several key challenges stand out to me that I try to address here.

First, as a field, we continue to remain siloed in ways that impede collaboration and result in fracturing our field's ability to garner the support, political will, attention, and resources that young children and families deserve. As researchers, we have each chosen specific areas to focus on: early literacy, early math, infant and toddler care, early childhood special education. These foci are important because they allow us to build the field's knowledge in each area of expertise. We try to make connections across our areas of expertise, hoping the mantle of "early childhood" will connect us. However, the field currently feels too fragmented for that to truly tie us together. Partly this is about resources. Having conducted research in Michigan and Ohio for the past 10 years, often comparing their very differently organized early childhood systems, I continually bump up against a stark reality—taking the small piece of the pie allotted to children and families by the federal government and states in the United States and trying to share it out to garner the "best" outcomes is largely a losing game. This model forces not only very difficult choices on children and families, who face very limited child care and early learning options, but also on local agencies, local and state governments, and individuals tasked with bridging these bodies. It also forces researchers in the field to try to seek research funding, programs, and other opportunities, often at the expense of other important initiatives. This is a very challenging reality that reinforces the silos in which we work, and make collaboration not just difficult but also unrealistic. Even of more import is that we have to start grounding our work in the lived experiences of practicing teachers, child care providers, families, and children. Too often the work of the field is dictated from the top down rather than the people who are living and working in the early childhood settings that are being studied, planned for, and/or targeted for policies.

Second, our focus has become too centered on child outcomes and the input/output model of measuring what we *should* be doing in early childhood spaces. This model assumes that if we can just figure out what experiences, styles of teaching, degree level of teachers, and/or environments (as just a few examples of inputs) result in the desired outcome, we can make all elements of early childhood align with these evidence-based practices, and garner the specific outcomes in different locations with different groups of children. The concern with this model is that it denies the agency and professional knowledge of practitioners, who can and should make decisions that they believe best support the needs of their students, sometimes contrary to what the evidence indicates is "best." I worry that as we continue to narrow what is "good" practice and "high-quality" teaching, we lose the benefits of diverse practitioners, with professional knowledge, making decisions that they believe best benefit their students. The focus has become measurable outcomes, and evidence of the impacts of intervention. Funding for Head Start programs, local child care agencies, school districts, and other federal programs has become predicated on measurable outcomes that often constrain the practices that we want teachers and caregivers to engage in with their work with young children. I worry that early childhood teachers focus their attention now on where they should be moving students, rather than on responding to and building knowledge with their students. This creates constrained and frustrating relationships for teachers and children. In talking with early years teachers, much of their concern focuses on requiring work of children that fails to account for developmental, cultural, and community differences. Early childhood teachers find themselves simultaneously pushed toward inclusivity and labeling children as "behind" before they barely begin. The stress isn't just among teachers. A rise in emotional and behavioral challenges in preschool and early elementary classrooms points to educational experiences that fail to value young children's social and emotional well-being above their academic performance. Many of my undergraduate students ask how to strike the right balance—to meet the expectations for academic progress (yes, even in pre-kindergarten programs) and also respond when children's social and emotional needs preclude academic instruction at the pace expected. My advice is to always start by building respect and connections with children that value their emotional needs, but this does not keep the academic expectations at bay. As a field, I think we are currently stuck, and we need to consider how we must change our approaches to truly make possible what we know young children deserve in early care and early elementary environments. We have been too focused on outcomes, at the expense of the real needs and lives of young children.

Finally, I worry that our focus on trying to prove that ECE is "worthy" of investment works against our efforts to have an early care and learning system that is accessible for all children and families who seek it. This idea that investment should be predicated on outcomes is deeply ableist, and assumes that children are only worthy of safe, responsive, and caring early learning environments *if*, in the future, they will be able to contribute to society. Children should be "invested in" simply because they are children—it is our responsibility to make opportunities for the most vulnerable in our society, not to decide that they are only deserving if the outcomes are convincing. Additionally, if we had a national system of available, accessible, supportive early care and learning, we might truly be able to evaluate what classroom environments, teacher practices, types of interactions, materials, and so on are actually impactful on children's social, emotional, and cognitive well-being.

Across the chapters in this book, the contributors to this book noted the complexities that make practice in early childhood spaces currently so difficult. Despite the recognition that children and families are participants in complex systems, our focus as a field has too often been on practices that seek to reduce (or ignore) the complexity of these systems. These attempts to limit these complexities deny the lived realities of young children and their families, and prevent us from valuing the cultural, linguistic, community, and family structures that make children's lives rich and real. We spend too much time trying to identify the deficits, rather than embracing the beauty that can be a part of the complicated realities in the lives of young children and their families. There is no silver bullet, no magical formula, no way to make the perfect intervention or teach the lessons by a script to get the desired results. It is not until we can meet the basic and fundamental needs of young children and their families in ways that embrace these complexities that we will be able to truly practice in ways that respond to and value the diversity of children's lives. What I propose feels radical, and somewhat impossible—and is in no way novel: Young children deserve supportive, inclusive, and responsive early care and learning environments and opportunities because of who they are now—fully human persons with rights.

This is the third challenge for our field: Early care and learning environments must be viewed and advocated for as a fundamental human right. Regardless of whether or not early care and learning programs directly impact children's 3rd-grade reading scores, children are still deserving of safe, supportive early care and learning environments. To me the rights argument must be primary, and the how-to-garner-outcomes argument must be secondary or tertiary. Children cannot have the outcomes that we want them to have if we are not able to give them the basic rights that they deserve. What comes next—how we educate teachers; define and enact quality environments; engage in continuous improvement; and teach children to read/count/analyze—cannot be truly studied and known until we achieve the basic human right of safe, supportive early care and learning environments for all children in the United States and other countries struggling to enact these realities.

I do not want this chapter to be all doom and gloom. Across my career so far, I have witnessed incredible changes to early care and learning systems that seek to provide more inclusive, supportive, and responsive opportunities for children and families. I continue to be deeply impressed by the commitments of early childhood policymakers and leaders in the states where I work. Their focus is truly on how to best meet the needs of children and families—within the real constraints of state budgets and shifting political priorities. Similarly, I have had the pleasure of spending time in classrooms with Head Start teachers and assistants; with kindergarten teachers and community-based preschool teachers; with family child care providers, intervention specialists, and social workers who show us how listening to, and valuing the perspectives of, children and families can create supportive, respectful and inclusive sites of early care and learning. All of us in this field—teachers, leaders, policymakers, researchers, and teacher educators—must truly seek to understand and recenter our efforts on what is real and important in our work—to recognize, respect, learn from, and respond to the needs of diverse populations of children, families, and early care professionals. When I am in early care and learning sites, I can also see how much more we could support the work of early care professionals, and meet the needs of children and families with diverse needs, realities, and experiences if we had the political and national will needed to guarantee early care and learning opportunities for all children as a fundamental human right.

While the field of early childhood has gained so much ground, the challenges that continue to face practitioners, families and children are daunting. In the United States, we continue to fail to meet the vast needs of families with young children who are seeking safe, reliable, accessible, and responsive care for children ages 0 to 5. We continue to identify, but largely fail to address, the ways in which poverty, trauma, and insecurity create barriers for children and families to live full, safe, and supported lives. We continue to struggle to address equity and fail to enact meaningful solutions and/or reconciliation for racial, ethnic, linguistic, (dis)ability, gender identity, and family configuration injustices. We fail to support the professional skills, knowledge, and practices of early childhood professionals who have come to care settings to work with children and families along varied pathways. We fail to ensure that early childhood professionals can support themselves and their own families on the incomes that they earn raising up other children and families. In the end, we do not yet fully value young children as having their own rights, and our responsibilities in meeting these rights.

So how do we change this? The work has to start small. We must begin with advocacy for universal child care opportunities in the United States. This means agreeing that all children, simply because they exist, have a right to supportive, responsive, and caring early care and learning provision. We also need to advocate for the mental health and well-being of children and teachers in early childhood and early elementary spaces, where too often expectations of what children "should" be doing take precedence over responding to and building on what children are doing. This also means trusting early childhood professionals to have agency and make decisions, rather than follow scripts or perform certain kinds of quality. We need to broaden our conceptions of quality in early childhood spaces to include cultural and community differences, to value family perspectives, and to let those voices participate in crafting what should and does happen in responsive early childhood spaces. We need to seek every policy avenue possible to support equitable and family-supporting pay for all sectors of early childhood education. We need to get political and garner attention to what we know young children and their families need from ages 0 to 5, to create a strong foundational experience for the rest of their lives. We need to counter the notion that children are widgets, and humanize the lived experience of families in diverse communities as they seek to access and engage with early care and learning opportunities for their young children. This is the incredibly challenging reality of early childhood education right now—how to ensure that children and families have not only their needs, but also their fundamental rights, met through the provision of safe, caring, supportive, and inclusive early learning environments that respect their complex identities and lived realities. I have hope, but recognize, too, that we have much work to do.

A Final Word on Conversations

Andrew J. Stremmel

In this book, we have employed a dialogic process of meaning-making. Conversations on the past, the present, and the future of what we believe to be critical issues in the field of early childhood education have enabled the voices of highly regarded experts to share their professional perspectives and concerns about the discourse driving early childhood education today.

But why conversations? To address this question, I turn to David Bohm's (1996) classic book, *On Dialogue,* which distinguishes dialogue from mere discussion, which tends toward analysis and "batting the ideas back and forth" in a competitive manner. Dialogue, by contrast, has creative and unifying effects, and is a cooperative endeavor that facilitates mutual exploration and truth-seeking. The conversations in this volume attempt to do just that. They involve active listening and reflection. They often involve personal storytelling as a means of making connections. And they provide an opportunity to reflect on perspectives regarding key issues in the field.

Reflection has always been an important disposition or stance in education, and each conversation has allowed the authors to reflect, often critically, on their conversations and to think about issues in a different way. This is important to break free from the prevailing efforts in traditional textbooks and research journals to frame the discourse to create a specific way of thinking about the issues brought up in this book. Through personal and meaningful dialogue on key topics in the field and their perceived impact on the past, present, and future of the field, we have endeavored to offer a more holistic and authentic space for readers to develop their own questions and strategies for continuing the conversation begun by expert leaders. We believe these conversations will allow readers to create new perspectives and understandings through ongoing reflection and continued dialogue necessary to advance our field and more hopefully embrace early childhood education that is more authentically and primarily about full human development. We invite you to continue the conversation.

REFERENCE

Bohm, D. (1996). *On dialogue*. Routledge.

Index

About the Editors

Nancy File is Professor Emerita at the University of Wisconsin-Milwaukee. She received her B.S. in Child Development/Child Care from the University of Pittsburgh. She earned both an M.S. and a Ph.D. from Purdue University with a focus, respectively, in Child Development and Early Childhood Education. She began her career teaching in child care and later spent several years as a teacher in two child development laboratory schools. Her research interests include children's classroom experiences during the preschool years. With colleagues, she has published *Curriculum in Early Childhood Education: Re-examined, Reclaimed, Renewed* (2011, 2020), *Understanding Research in Early Childhood Education* (2016, 2024), and *The Wiley Handbook of Early Childhood Care and Education* (2019). She serves on the editorial boards of the *Early Childhood Research Quarterly* and *Journal of Early Childhood Teacher Education.*

Nancy E. Barbour is Professor Emeritus at Kent State University's College of Education, Health, and Human Services. She received her Ph.D. in Human Development and Family Studies from The Pennsylvania State University, her M.Ed. in education from Wichita State University, and her B.A. in English from the University of Pennsylvania. She was a faculty member and associate dean at Kent State University in the College of Education, Health, and Human Services. Her research has focused on the preparation of the early childhood workforce, particularly within child development laboratory schools in university settings. She serves on the editorial boards of *Early Education and Development,* the *European Early Childhood Education Research Journal,* and the *International Journal of Early Education.* She served on the NAEYC Higher Education Accreditation Commission for 8 years. She was co-editor of the *Sage Handbook of Early Childhood Policy* (2018). The AERA Early Education/Child Development SIG awarded her the 2020 Distinguished Contribution to Early Education/Child Development Research Award.

Andrew J. Stremmel is Professor Emeritus in the School of Education, Counseling, and Human Development and former department head in Teaching, Learning and Leadership in the College of Education and Human Sciences at South Dakota State University. He received both his Ph.D. and M.S. degrees from Purdue University in Early Childhood Education and Child Development and earned his B.A. in psychology from the Pennsylvania State University. He has published widely in the areas of teacher as researcher, and Reggio Emilia–inspired, inquiry-based approaches to early childhood teacher education and curriculum. His co-authored book, *Teaching as Inquiry: Rethinking Curriculum in Early Childhood Education* (2005), is the first comprehensive early childhood education text provoked and inspired by the Reggio Emilia approach. He is an executive editor of *Voices of Practitioners*. In 2016 he received the Distinguished Research Award of the Association of Teacher Education for his co-authored article "Countering the Essentialized Discourse of Teacher Education" [*Journal of Early Childhood Teacher Education, 2015*].